# A JOURNEY TO A
## Spirit-Filled
## LIFE

DR. TERESITA "TESS" PAJE, MBA, DBS

innovo
PUBLISHING

Published by Innovo Publishing, LLC
www.innovopublishing.com
1-888-546-2111

**innovo**
PUBLISHING

Providing Full-Service Publishing Services for Christian Authors, Artists &
Ministries: Books, eBooks, Audiobooks, Music, Screenplays, Film & Curricula

A JOURNEY TO A SPIRIT-FILLED LIFE

ISBN: 978-1-61314-784-9

Cover Design & Interior Layout: Innovo Publishing, LLC

Printed in the United States of America
U.S. Printing History
First Edition: 2021

Has God called you to create a Christian book, eBook, audiobook, music album,
screenplay, film, or curricula? If so, visit the ChristianPublishingPortal.com to learn
how to accomplish your calling with excellence. Learn to do everything yourself, or
hire trusted Christian Experts from our Marketplace to help.

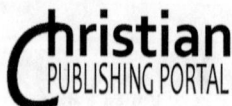

**christian**
PUBLISHING PORTAL

# Contents

# Introduction

In our journey heavenward, we should expect more detours with the passage of time. But Hebrews 13:5 says, *"For He Himself has said, 'I will never leave you nor forsake you.'"* Despite everyday challenges, setbacks, personal struggles, and emotional traumas that we go through, this verse confirms God's promise that in being a true believer, we shall have the gracious presence of God in life, at death, and forever. We must be confident that there is assurance of help from God, *"So we may boldly say, 'The Lord is my helper; I will not fear what can man do to me"* (Heb 13:6).

After my first book, I would have never imagined writing about my continuing journey. Nonetheless, God has already begun a good work in me such that my faithfulness and obedience to Him paved the way to a more purposeful and godly mission. Indeed, He has continued to open many more doors of opportunities for me to proclaim His love, mercy, and grace. These unsurpassed manifestations of God into my life and to the lives of my family, friends, and others are all presented in this book. What was revealed to me by God in His plan for my life indeed became real. In this next journey, mission take-off is where God's many missions began to unfold. Exalting His name, upholding His promises, and yielding to His path would give a solemn declaration that the so-called mysteries are no longer mysteries, and the miracles are no longer miracles—but these are all true, and Jesus' plan is for real. Unparalleled events that happened in my life far exceeded my hopes and dreams; they were all truly answered prayers. They are true witnesses of what our living God can and will do for us; thus all praises, honors, and glories belong to our heavenly Father.

As I share this episode of my journey, I trust that this book will be used by God and will minister to readers. The book contains Scriptures that bring knowledge and understanding as I related them to actual life situations. It reintroduces and reinforces biblical principles and practices to guide and illuminate our paths so we will not stumble or fall. In this book, the sequences of the chapters were designed to create a step-by-step process into our journey as we continually discern God's calling.

*Chapter 1: Step One* asks the question, *How well do we know our relationships?* (To God:) It helps us to focus on the nature of God, the importance of God's Word, and the power of prayer, and then it walks us to our salvation and repentance as we become rightly related to Him. (To ourselves:) It helps us evaluate who we are and see ourselves as Jesus would see us. (To others:) It helps us understand the true meaning of loving one another. The Ten Commandments in Exodus 20:1-17 were incorporated in this chapter as a great admonisher to abide by the Law of God. Matthew 22:37–40 was also exemplified in this chapter: "You shall love the LORD your God with all your heart, with all your soul, and with all your mind. This is the first and great commandment. And the second is like it: 'You shall love your neighbor as yourself. On these two commandments hang all the Law and the Prophets.'" It emphasizes the completeness of the kind of love believers must have for God. For the same reason, it reminds believers to ascertain their love for others by what they wish for themselves. These moral duties to God, to ourselves, and to others will carry us into a greater realm.

*Chapter 2: Step Two* asks the question, *Are we dreamers?* It encourages us to be dreamers not only for ourselves but for others as we seek God's revelation. It allows us to envision things that are of God through our faith. For the Bible says nothing is impossible for Him. As we bring forth our dreams/vision into reality, then *Chapter 3: Step Three* leads us to the question, *Can we make a difference?* Sure we can, as we learn how to step out of our comfort zone into our faith zone, a new realm of life doing things for God that will enable us to help others and society.

Stay focused on Him as *Chapter 4: Step Four* asks this question: *Are we living our lives to full capacity?* It focuses our allegiance to living a godly life and finding God's purpose in light of the storms of life. As we read *Chapter 5: Step Five*, the question, *Are we moving on as Christians?* is explored. If we are "running the race of faith," then we are. It portrays how well we obey God's truth and our faithfulness to Him. By being obedient and faithful to God, we could be "unleashing our potential to lead." At all times, we must be in alignment with God's plan for our lives.

In conclusion, the final step in *Chapter 6: Step Six* asks us, *Are we bound for heaven?* I certainly hope we are.

This series of rhetorical questions enables us to gain biblical understanding and godly insights as it opens up our hearts to a greater degree of godly influence. Drawing from the life of Jesus as a true leader and His great examples and teachings, I certainly trust that we emulate them. I hope and pray that when God calls you to come away with Him for a sacred time of spiritual renewal that you are obedient. Indeed, I was.

In this book, I also share with you my personal prayers, testimonies, and convictions attesting to my obedience to His call. I sincerely hope that these godly insights will inspire you and add spice to your everyday life as you interact with your personal and godly reflections.

It is therefore my fervent hope and prayer that this book will carry readers to a greater level of understanding God's Word and the forever truth behind everything that was said about Jesus and His life, examples, and teachings. Jesus' manifestations into my life and to the lives of those in my circle of influence are representations of Jesus' presence in all of us. We must continue to seek His kingdom and be rightly related to Him, for *"Jesus Christ is the same yesterday, today and forevermore"* (Heb 13:8).

A significant occurrence in my life was added and highlighted to supplement this book: "My Personal Conviction as a Woman of God." It's about my very personal struggle in my marriage that almost destroyed my family relationship. Indeed, the Lord convicted my heart to share this, especially with women just like me who are battling with the leadership role in today's Christian families. This struggle brought about a chain of unprecedented predicaments, but with God's intervention and His amazing grace, our relationship was restored.

This is the dilemma: it is when husbands do not like to lead and become uninvolved or sometimes unpredictable about their role as "head of the family." This has been a big issue in my family since the beginning of our marriage. I never felt my husband's interest to lead the family. So I decided to handle all the responsibilities by myself. I never complained about it until it became a problem, which prompted even bigger problems. I hope and pray that my poignant testimonies of pain and endurance will be a learning opportunity for those who read it. It is my intention that by sharing this publicly, it will open up many people's hearts to acknowledge and become aware of the impact leadership roles have in a family relationship. My goal is to give hope and encouragement. I deeply and wholeheartedly pray for women who struggle in this to seek guidance because I strongly believe there's a way out. My message is meant to save your marriage and help you sustain a healthy relationship. Help is on the way; I know because it is *God's way.*

This book is not meant to merely share my personal calling and convictions but also to share what God can do for anyone who wants to understand and live his or her Christian life to the fullest.

I pray you experience a real thrill in your adventure with God. Just as I did, you're bound to make mistakes along the way. Those mistakes should encourage us to depend more on God and trust that He will help us. It is also my fervent prayer that on our journey, we bring people with us to finish the race and receive our heavenly prize. Please pray this prayer with me:

*J—Jesus, as we journey together*
*O—Open our hearts to the truth*
*U—Underlying Your kingdom pursuit*
*R—Running the race of faith, which is a*
*N—Never-ending process, but . . .*
*E—Eternal life in heaven we will achieve, and*
*Y—Yielding to you, Father, will end the quest.*
*Amen.*

## STEP ONE

# How Well Do We Know Our Relationships?

The purpose of this chapter is to provide knowledge and understanding of our relationship to God, to ourselves, and to others. Building our relationship with God is an integral part of becoming a Christian. Thus *Step One* is the foundational step in beginning our journey with God. The key themes of this step include discovering God's nature and attributes, discovering the importance of God's Word, discovering the power of prayer, and walking our way to salvation and repentance. It is my fervent prayer that as we begin this first step of our journey, the Holy Spirit will dwell in our hearts so that we gain wisdom, understanding, and spiritual guidance in the five steps that follow.

## Our Relationships to God

For His own purpose and glory, God created the universe. Thus He has the ultimate control of everything. However, God gave men freedom to be able to decide things for themselves. Romans 3:23 says, *"For all have sinned and fall short of the glory of God,"* but God loves us, and He restores us from our fallen nature. Indeed, God is both our Creator and redeemer. The foundation of our knowledge about God rests upon our desire to know His nature, and knowing His nature will create in us a deeper understanding of who He is in our life and what His will and purpose is for us. I believe learning and understanding some of the Scriptures underlying God's nature will bring truth into our hearts.

God is present everywhere in the universe at the same time. We call Him omnipresent. Therefore, He sees everything that is happening. *"For He looks to the ends of the earth, And sees under the whole heavens"* (Jb 28:24). This Scripture shows that God knows all about our sufferings because He sees all things, and only true wisdom belongs to God, our Creator. *"For you have trusted in your wickedness; You have said, 'No one sees me'; Your wisdom and your knowledge have warped you; And you have said in your heart, 'I am and there is no one else besides me'"* (Is 47:10). This Scripture refers to sinners who think they are safe because nobody sees their wickedness, and there is none to judge them. But be on guard because God is watchful.

God being the Creator of everything, He is all-powerful. We call Him omnipotent. He has an unlimited power and authority. *"For the word of God is living and powerful, and sharper than any two-edged sword, piercing even to the division of soul and spirit, and of joints and marrow, and is a discerner of the thoughts and intents of the heart"* (Heb 4:12). God is in control of everything and has the power to bring us to eternal judgment. God's Word is living and powerful, and while it nourishes our spiritual body and comforts our heart, it may also be used for our judgment.

God fills the heavens and the earth, and He knows everything. We call Him omniscient. He has an infinite knowledge and understanding about our lives. *"For if our heart condemns us, God is greater than our heart, and knows all things"* (1 Jn 3:20). Because of the greatness of God, He knows who His followers are, and He wants to assure salvation in them, but He also knows those who do not follow Him. *"And there is no creature hidden from His sight, but all things are naked and open to the eyes of Him to whom we must give account"* (Heb 4:13). Each individual has a place in God's eyes; thus each of us is being judged by Him. We are accountable both to the living God and to the Word of God.

Our knowledge and understanding about God and His character will significantly tie the cord of our relationship with God. God's love is unconditional as fully revealed in the life and death of Jesus, and He is merciful to protect sinners from what they deserve. God is full of grace; His undeserved favor is revealed through Jesus Christ's redemptive sufferings and death on the cross for the forgiveness of our sins through our faith.

The Old Testament stresses that there is only one God. But God reveals Himself as three "persons" with different functions. When we call upon God, we use different names: Father, Son (Jesus), and Holy Spirit. We call God our Father because of His relationship to Jesus, the eternal Son. Our union with Jesus brought us to share that intimate relationship between the Father and the Son. Then we call unto Jesus, the Son of God, who was obedient under the authority of His Father. John 3:16 says, *"For God so loved the world that He gave His only begotten Son, that whoever believes in Him should not perish but have everlasting life."* Lastly, we call upon the Holy Spirit who was sent from the Father in Jesus' name. Jesus was once alive and lived with us, but now the Spirit lives in us. *"But you are not in the flesh but in the*

*Spirit, if indeed the Spirit of God dwells in you. Now if anyone does not have the Spirit of Christ, he is not His"* (Rom 8:9). This Scripture tells us that the Spirit of God lives in us only if we trust in Jesus Christ; otherwise, we can never claim Jesus as our Lord and Savior.

The following verses bear witness to all three persons—Father, Son (Jesus), and Holy Spirit—and their involvement throughout our lives. Jesus said, *"I and My Father are one"* (Jn 10:30). Both the Father and the Son are committed to our protection and safety. *"Jesus answered, 'If anyone loves Me, he will keep My word; and My Father will love him, and We will come to him and Make our home with him'"* (Jn 14:23). We have to be obedient to God's Word as evidence of our love to the Father and the Son whose unconditional love is manifested into our heart. Jesus, the Son of God, lives in us from the moment we acknowledge Him as our Savior and accept Him as our Lord.

In as much as our body needs physical nourishment, it also needs spiritual nourishment. Ephesians 1:13 says, *"In Him you also trusted, after you heard the word of truth, the gospel of your salvation; in whom also, having believed, you were sealed with the Holy Spirit of promise."* Hearing the Word of God, trusting in Him, and believing in the gospel of Jesus Christ will bring salvation, and by faith, we belong to God and possess the Holy Spirit. The Spirit who dwells in us produces fruit, as Paul declared to the Galatians. *"But the fruit of the Spirit is love, joy, peace, patience, kindness, goodness, faithfulness, gentleness, and self-control"* (Gal 5:22–23).

Having the desire to be deeply rooted to the foundational knowledge and understanding of God's nature and character, we draw closer to God. In drawing closer to God, we ponder these essential obligations: first, we must receive God's Word exactly for what it is; second, we must honor God's Word; and lastly, we must obey God's Word. It does not end there because our personal relationship with

God resides within those obligations. That means we need to trust God personally as well as believe the truth about Him and live a life in harmony with Him. Our lives were given to us by God; therefore, we must be dependent upon Him and His promises. Living for God means putting all your energy into serving and pleasing Him. This does not necessarily mean that we all have to serve in the mission field, but we are to become the best we can be with the talents, gifts, and abilities given to us by God. I can say,

I *received God's Word* through His amazing grace.

I *honor God's Word* with allegiance in His truth.

I *obey God's Word,* for they are His commands and promises.

I am so thankful and grateful for all the great wonders that God has blessed me with after I accepted Jesus into my life as my Lord and Savior. Looking back, I have come to realize that all the challenges and struggles I went through were part of my awakening call. I was filled with an unforgiving heart, I harbored anger, and I was swarmed with unimaginable resentments and frustrations. Because of the lies and deception in my marital relationship, I became relentless, unrealistic, and ungodly in my disposition. The pain that lingered continued to persist until I learned how to forgive. If I had hardened my heart to the Lord, I could have missed out on His divine calling. There were many more confirmations affirming that those years of affliction were the beginning of His revelations into my life.

In my first book, I shared how God's divine intervention came along when I underwent a family relational problem. God revealed to me the power to forgive; thus my faith in Him was strengthened, as I was able to move forward in my life. During this process, God's grace and mercy redeemed me from the bondage of my unforgiving heart.

> *Prayer for God's Mercy:*
> *F—Forgive me of my iniquities*
> *O—O Jesus, my Savior and my Lord*
> *R—Restore my heart and soul*
> *G—Grant me the power to forgive*
> *I—Instill in my heart the*
> *V—Victory to proclaim*
> *E—Everlasting love and peace*

This verse in Romans 12:2 brought a new perspective in my life: *"And do not be conformed to this world, but be transformed by the renewing of your mind, that you may prove what is that good and acceptable and perfect will of God."* By redirecting my life to God, my outlook in life changed. I learned to forgive my husband's infidelity, and it was the beginning of many more profound changes in our marital relationship. After my husband asked forgiveness from God and accepted Jesus as his Lord and Savior, my healing process began. Colossians 3:13 says, *"Make allowance for each other's faults, and forgive anyone who offends you. Remember, the Lord forgave you, so you must forgive others."* With my aching heart, God empowered me to forgive not just my husband but also other people who had wronged me.

God also dealt with the direction of my career path to become a financial advisor. Through this career, I became a mentor—financial and life planning—to many people. With God's great command, I became obedient and started sharing the gospel with others.

God truly prepared me to rediscover my compassion for people. He reignited my compassion to work with them, which later became my passion to serve the Lord. Awakened by the truth about God and His amazing grace, never again did I dwell on what went wrong in the tarnished relationship that almost derailed my journey. God always intervened as I called on Him and claimed His promises.

I also realized that God never left me, and He already had set plans for me. God's plan for me is real. His great love enabled me to open my heart to a brighter and more purposeful future, paving the way to my journey heavenward. These passages from Jeremiah 29:11-13 became my stronghold: *"'For I know the thoughts that I think toward you,' says the Lord, 'thoughts of peace and not of evil, to give you a future and a hope. Then you will call upon Me and go and pray to Me, and I will listen to you. And you will seek Me and find Me, when you search for Me with all your heart.'"* Many more good things will take place as I testify to God's presence in my everyday walk with Him. God is always with us, and I know that we can be used by Him no matter where we find ourselves.

Praise His holy name, and to God be the glory in all the things we do, through our faith and work that cannot be separated. That makes us true Christians with our faith in Jesus, our great redeemer, as testified by these two passages: Luke 9:23–24 says, *"If any of you wants to be my follower, you must turn from your selfish ways, take up your cross daily, and follow me. If you try to hang on to your life, you will lose it. But if you give up your life for my sake, you will save it."* Romans 10:9 also says, *"That if you confess with your mouth the Lord Jesus and believe in your heart that God has raised Him from the dead, you will be saved."*

God's Word reveals three aspects of His will for all of us: His will of purpose (God's plan), His will of desire (our salvation), and His will of command (obey Him). Remember these three things:

1. His will of purpose—God has a wonderful plan for us to be in fellowship with Him.

2. His will of desire—God will redeem us if we accept Jesus as our Lord and Savior.

3. His will of command—We must be obedient to God's commands and promises.

With that being said, we are now ready to discover, through God's Word, His promises and how God holds us secure in His love throughout our journey heavenward.

# God's Word

The Bible is God's eternal Word. It was said in Hebrews 4:12, *"For the word of God is alive and powerful. It is sharper than the sharpest two-edged sword, cutting between soul and spirit, between joint and marrow. It exposes our innermost thoughts and desires."* As you spend time studying and meditating on God's Word, I pray you will experience power from God that will expose your inner beliefs and intentions. The Word of God becomes comfort and nourishment to those who believe and a tool of judgment to those who have not committed themselves to Jesus.

God's Word is full of promises, and they are unbreakable promises to help us in many ways. We would never know what the future holds for us, but with God's promises of support, His guidance, and His presence, He holds us secure in His love throughout this life. When we face difficulty or temptation, we must cling onto God's promise of support, and we will receive it just as much as when life is smooth sailing.

Experiencing life challenges can often become an opportunity to feel God's power working in us. My challenges in life brought forth my total dependency upon God's promises. He enabled me to conquer all my inhibitions, infirmities, indifference, illness, and everything that was not in accordance with His will for me, just like what He promised in Romans 8:37: *"Yet in all these things we are more than conquerors through Him who loved us."*

Trusting His great love gave me a higher level of intimacy in my personal relationship with God. Three major struggles prompted me to become more obedient and faithful to Him. First, my marital relationship, which was once wrecked by infidelity, became a wake-up call for me and my husband to come back to God. Second, people prying their noses into my personal and family affairs for over a decade as they continually harassed me, inflicted a lingering pain, fear, anger, and frustration in my life. My health was severely affected, but with God's promise of guidance, I gained the strength and power to forgive. Lastly, working in corporate America, where politicking left people heartless, made me call unto God's promise of His presence. I quit my old job, and not long afterward, I found a better job as a financial advisor.

God promises to be with everyone everywhere who loves and serves Him. *"Teaching them to observe all things that I have commanded you; and lo, I am with you always, even to the end of the age. Amen"* (Mt 28:20). What a remarkable promise, even to the end of the age. Indeed, I conquered and survived all of my dilemmas. God taught me great lessons that in the end, His promises became visible, and His love became more invincible. God's love is sufficient enough to get me to the next level of understanding His Word.

The Bible has a cleansing effect in our daily walk with Him. The Holy Spirit uses the Bible to broaden our godly vision and to strengthen our faith. The Bible also guides us to find our way in life as God intended. Through the Holy Spirit, the Word of God can be imparted to our body, mind, soul, and spirit as it will be reflected in our character and personalities. Indeed, the Word of God is true yesterday, today, and forevermore. His promises in the Bible are true, His love for us is unconditional and perfect, and His plan for our lives is real. Thus each time we read the Word of God, it should give us the confidence to tackle life head on.

## PERSONAL REFLECTION

I would like you to reflect for a moment on what you did when you needed God the most in your life. Please answer these questions from your heart.

1. Did you resort to reading the Bible and meditating upon God's Word?

2. Did you encounter God's promises of support and guidance and His presence?

3. How often do you read and study the Bible?

4. I believe that the Bible is our love letter from God. Do you feel the same way?

5. Do you also realize and believe that God's plan in your life is for real?

Likely, if you were not accustomed to reading and meditating upon His Word, especially when you needed Him the most, it could be a great challenge. I was in that position before I began to establish my personal relationship with the Lord. Needless to say, it is not too late; you can start now. Begin reading and meditating upon God's Word, and invite God into your heart to live with you. Revelation 3:20 says, *"Behold, I stand at the door and knock. If anyone hears My voice and opens the door, I will come in to him and dine with him, and he with Me."*

Now, be ready as we embark on what I hope to be a defining moment in your life—needing to accept Jesus into your life or renewing your personal relationship with Him. We are just about ready to encounter a life-changing journey heavenward.

## Our Salvation

God truly loves us, and He has great plans for our lives. His greatest plan is to rescue us from our rebellion and disobedience so we can be set free from the bondage of our sins. The death of Jesus Christ was the means by which God has dealt with our sins. And in order to become a follower of Christ, or be called a Christian, we need to do our part; we must repent and abandon our old ways, and through the Holy Spirit, we will be forgiven. When we repent and believe in Christ, the Holy Spirit also enters our life. Read and reflect on the following verses that will lead you to your salvation as you begin to experience the fullness of God.

All of us have sinned and deserve God's righteous wrath, but He sent His Son, Jesus, who was sinless, for the propitiation of our sins and satisfying God's wrath, that we may know Him, have a relationship with Him, and have eternal life. Once we fully comprehend what God did for us, we become humble and seek God's eternal kingdom and a holy life. Romans 3:23 says, *"For all have sinned and fall short of the glory of God."* And in Romans 6:23, *"For the wages of sin is death, but the gift of God is eternal life in Christ Jesus our Lord."* But then Romans 10:9-11 clearly states, *"That if you confess with your mouth the Lord Jesus and believe in your heart that God raised Him from the dead, you will be saved. For with the heart one believes unto righteousness and with the mouth confession is made unto salvation."*

When we truly believe in our hearts that we are saved, we begin to enjoy and experience life in a totally new way. Second Corinthians 5:17-18 says, *"Therefore, if anyone is in Christ, he is a new creation; old things have passed away; behold, all things have become new. Now all things are of God, who has reconciled us to Himself through Jesus Christ, and has given us the ministry of reconciliation."* Having been saved is a grace from God. Grace is the free, unearned favor from God. We don't deserve this gift, even if we are doing good works or on our best behavior. But all we have to do is accept Jesus' call to repentance, which means to turn from the old ways toward His call to faith, which means to turn toward God and believe in Him.

Second Peter 3:9 says, *"The Lord isn't really being slow about his promise, as some people think. No, he is being patient for your sake. He does not want anyone to be destroyed, but wants everyone to repent."* Then God's promise of forgiveness and gift of the Spirit will be made available to us. The promise of forgiveness means the beginning of a new way of life, and the gift of the Spirit gives us power to serve Him and the assurance of eternal life. Through the saving power of Jesus Christ, or what we call our salvation, we are now reconciled with God. When we get to reconcile with God, we begin to establish our personal relationship with Him.

## PERSONAL REFLECTION

Pause for a moment and reflect in your heart if you are now ready to accept Jesus as your Lord and Savior. If so, congratulations! Please pray with me the prayer of salvation written below. This could now be the beginning of a new day for you to experience the fullness of God in your life. And as you become rightly related to Him, your outlook in life could change, and the direction of your life could yield into that of God's will and purpose. On the other hand, if you believe that your life is a very slow work in progress, or you simply need to renew your relationship with Jesus, then I invite you all to pray with me this simple prayer:

> *Prayer of Salvation*
> *"Lord Jesus, I acknowledge that I am a sinner; please forgive me. I want to open my heart for You to come in and live with me to be my personal Lord and Savior. Thank You for dying on the cross to rescue me from all of my sins. I now commit my life to You today to be worthy of Your kingdom purpose. And*

*by the power of Your Holy Spirit, I now receive the
assurance of eternal life. Amen."*

# Repentance

In Luke 5:32, Jesus said, *"I have not come to
call the righteous, but sinners, to repentance."* Repentance is
being deeply sorry for your sin; it involves a change of mind
and heart, leading to a change in action. After we realize
that we have broken God's laws, acknowledge that we have
gone astray, and want to put things right, we repent. It is a
willingness to change your old life and have a clean break of
the past. Through our faith, we turn to God for forgiveness,
but first we have to know that Jesus died for our sins and
believe in our heart that this is true. Therefore, we accept
Him as our Lord and Savior. We are also given the ordinance
of baptism as a sign that our old life was changed into new
life.

In becoming a Christian, as we repent and abandon our
old way of life, God will forgive us and empower us through
the Holy Spirit. The Holy Spirit gives us a new nature and new
perspective in life. Through repentance, we are reconciled to
God through Jesus. Our aim should be to confess each of our
sins all throughout life. We must trust in God and draw on
His power. Following are the Ten Commandments as listed
in Exodus 20:1-17. They are the core teachings regarding our
relationship with God and with one another.

*The Ten Commandments*

1.  I am the Lord your God.
2.  You shall have no other gods before Me.
3.  You shall not make for yourself a carved image.
4.  You shall not take the name of the Lord your God
    in vain.

5. Honor your father and your mother.

6. You shall not murder.

7. You shall not commit adultery.

8. You shall not steal.

9. You shall not bear false witness against your neighbor.

10. You shall not covet your neighbor's house.

# Prayer

We must learn how to pray in order to experience the fullness of our communion with God. When we pray, the Holy Spirit makes intercession for us. In order to understand the true test of spirituality, I personally believe that it can only be manifested through the reading of God's Word and prayer. We won't know exactly how to pray unless we know what the Bible teaches us about God, His will, and His purpose. The study of God's Word creates a meaningful prayer life, so much so that it helps us understand God's truth—truth that will speak to us when we open up our hearts to God and commune with Him. Indeed, prayer is one of the most vital subjects of Christian life.

When we pray, we humbly and willingly submit to God's plans and purposes for our lives. We honor, praise, and glorify God as we invite Him to dwell within our hearts. Allow God to have His way, as we become in perfect union with Him. Prayer is very important in our relationship with God. It is our way of communicating with Him and trusting His will for us. Through our prayers, we come to know better our Father in heaven. We can just be ourselves before Him, present our requests to God, and allow Him to come to us through our faith and prayers. Though He does not always change things for us, God does change us in the way we look at things. What we pray, where we pray, and how we pray should all be centered to God's will and purpose.

Philippians 4:6 says, *"Do not be anxious about anything, but in everything, by prayer and petition, with thanksgiving, present your requests to God."* When we become anxious for anything, it indicates our lack of trust in God's power and wisdom. Anxiety can distract us from God's plan. Therefore, instead of becoming agitated or worried, we should present everything to God with a petition and with prayers of thanksgiving. Our true prayers must be accompanied by our gratitude to God, with a spirit of thankfulness in His sovereignty, and then we will find our anxiety replaced with a spiritual peace. As we begin to pray from our heart, we become less focused on the demands of the world, and very likely, our focus is then centered on God.

Jesus gave us a pattern for how to pray. It is not to be merely recited or repeated, but every word of it should be spoken wholeheartedly, and with power from the Holy Spirit, we can lead godly lives. Let's read and meditate on this model prayer our heavenly Father taught us in Matthew 6:9-13.

*Our Father in heaven,*
*Hallowed be Your name.*
*Your kingdom come.*
*Your will be done*
*On earth as it is in heaven.*
*Give us this day our daily bread.*
*And forgive us our debts,*
*As we forgive our debtors.*
*And do not lead us into temptation,*
*But deliver us from the evil one.*
*For Yours is the kingdom and the power and the*
*glory forever. Amen.*

This model prayer is clearly notable for its simplicity and comprehensiveness. It's very clear how this prayer was directed to God and His kingdom and toward human needs. But as believers, we are to come out with our own words of worship, praise, and intercession before our Father in our prayers, not to merely recite or repeat this pattern of prayer Jesus gave us. We need to be warned against meaningless repetition. Matthew 6:7 says, *"And when you pray, do not use vain repetitions."* We also need to understand that Jesus is not forbidding us from repetition of prayer, but we need to make sure that our prayer is sincere and honest. It is the mindless, indifferent repeating that is not pleasing to God. He wants our hearts and our minds fully engaged every time we approach God in prayer.

Prayer is the most testifying evidence of our faith to the truth about God, His Word, and His promises. By our prayer, we are instructing ourselves to draw closer to Him and not Him to us. It determines our obedience and faithfulness to God's kingdom. Without prayer, there is no plan, passion, or purpose. It is therefore a privilege to approach God with a sincere heart with our plan, purpose, and devotion through prayer. Although He already knows everything about us, God is delighted to commune with us. Making known to Him our heart's desires, needs, burdens, and concerns allows God to intervene and reveal His nature and attributes. My understanding of prayers in the Scriptures truly equipped me with wisdom and direction to face the reality of everyday challenges. We must always pray to God; it is a significant representation of the unbroken cord of God's promises.

Oftentimes, though, we get caught up in the busyness of life, and we tend to forget to pray. Prayer became a very important part of me. It also broadened my perspectives on issues that used to bother me, especially with things that related to my family and workplace. Through the power of prayer, it lifted much of the weight I had on my shoulders as I carried around the burdens of every day. What truly binds us with God is our relationship with Him, our faith, our trust, and our love for Him. The true success in this relationship is to live under the authority of communication to our God through our endless prayers as we lay out our life openly to Him, open our hearts for Him to come in, and be truly dependent upon His will for us. After all, our ultimate purpose for prayer is to glorify God.

I would like to share with you my personal insight on the importance of prayer. Praying every day became a priority in my life. My husband and I make sure that we spend time together praying and reading our daily devotional book. We pray for many reasons: for people, purpose, problems, provision, protection, and praises. I have a list of prayer requests from all over the world. Indeed, there have been many answered prayers attesting to God's promises that manifested in our life and in the lives of our friends and others. Praises, honors, and glories to God as we exalt Him through prayer.

In fact, I just started a ministry project called Women of Great Purpose International where I addressed the issue of people needing to pray and to be prayed for. With this ministry, we targeted everyone around the world to join us in prayer. This is just one of the many objectives of this project. The availability of modern technology will make this mission accessible to many people all around the world. Henceforth, this is my prayer:

> *Heavenly Father,*
> *May this ministry bring vision*
> *To be carried throughout the nation*
> *May the purpose of prayer be delivered*
> *To all people as they pray and are prayed for.*
> *Amen*

## PERSONAL REFLECTION

Now we know that through salvation, we can be reconciled to God. It is the beginning of our personal relationship with Jesus. The Holy Spirit empowers us to do the things that glorify God. Through our prayers and reading the Word of God, we begin to experience the fullness of God. Reflect on how you can incorporate them into your life so you can experience the fullness of your communion with God by answering the following questions:

1. Do you read and meditate on God's Word?

2. How much time do you spend in prayer?

3. Do you make sufficient time and space away from distractions so that you can be open to God?

4. How does prayer help you?

5. Do you pray for others?

6. Have you or have you not started your daily habit of praying?

Praise God if you have. For others, maybe you lack the confidence to boldly and openly speak to God. If so, I would like to invite you to pray with me this simple prayer that I personalized for you:

> *Almighty Father, I give You the honor, praise, and glory, for today is another day to bring my own life before Your presence. I ask Your Holy Spirit to speak to my heart through Your Word so that I may hear what You have to say. Strengthen my faith to cling to Your promises of support and guidance and Your promise to be with everyone everywhere who loves and serves You. Forgive me of my iniquities so I can make peace to everyone as I pray for them also. May You provide nourishment to my physical and spiritual needs. And may Your will be done in me,*

*through me, and within me. These I pray in Jesus'*
*name, Amen.*

# Our Relationships to Ourselves

Having been saved through God's grace is the beginning
of our personal relationship with Him. And by the power of
God's love, we are called sons of the living God and brought
into His family. Being a member of God's family, how well
do we know ourselves? If we could just open up to God and
ask Him to tell us who we are, it would be a lot easier because
He will help us discern our own life. But if we are not rightly
related to Him, how can we relate to God's perspectives
and His revelation? It is only God's love that will help us
see within ourselves without guilt, shame, condemnation, or
fear. Therefore, understanding God's love for us will unleash
us from bondage. It could be self-deceiving to think that you
are doing well when in reality you hate things about yourself.
It is important to have a healthy relationship with yourself
before you can have a healthy relationship with God and
with others.

Matthew 7:3-5 says, *"And how can you look at the speck*
*in your brother's eye, but not consider the plank in your own eye.*
*Or how can you say to your brother, 'Let me remove the speck*
*from your eye'; and look, a plank is in your own eye? Hypocrite!*
*First remove the plank from your own eye, and then you will see*
*clearly to remove the speck from your brother's eye."* This teaches
us about an erroneous view we may have of ourselves. Before
we can point out the sins of another, we must first confess
our own sins. We could be blinded by the very nature of
self-righteousness and by a condemning spirit toward others.
Therefore, we need to ask for God's cleansing so we can see
everything more clearly—God, others, and ourselves. Let
God be the only judge and others as needy sinners just like
us. First, let's get our lives in alignment with God before we

can honestly and truly see ourselves, and then let God change us from inside out. Once we recognize our imperfections and confess them to God for forgiveness, then we can be rightly related to God and ourselves. God is faithful and just to forgive us from our sins and cleanse us from all unrighteousness, so allow Him to do a work in you.

We would like to assess and see ourselves as Jesus would see us. What would we like Jesus to see in us? Is it something He would be proud of, or would it edify Him? Do you think God sees you as a spiritual person, a sinful person, a saved person, or an unsaved person? To be a spiritual person, God gave us the ability to live in harmony with Him and to become whatever He intended us to be. We were born sinners, and for this reason, Jesus died for us to redeem us from all our sins. It is easy to fall into our old ways, but Jesus is a forgiving God. However, we must ask for forgiveness. We are saved the moment we receive Jesus into our lives as our Lord and Savior. It can be the beginning of a continuous experience of the fullness of God in our lives. For those who are unsaved, they just might not know the Lord, uniformed of His plan for mankind or mainly stubborn to receive Jesus into their lives. As a member of the family of God, we need to share the gospel with them and boldly speak of God's love and plan for them.

God is a person with whom we can have a lasting, growing relationship of love and trust. Through His Son, Jesus, He became man to be with us even for a short time. The Bible has many accounts of His love, plan, commands, and promises for us. He is a holy God made perfect in Himself. He is also a loving God, for His love is pure and unconditional. For our sake and for His purpose, He continually made known to us that He has specific things for us to do, whether we use our spiritual gifts to help people or we are used as an instrument to make a difference in the lives of many.

Unfortunately, many people do not realize what God has given them, which illustrates the importance of walking with God. We have to be aware of His presence in us, always keeping Him in our minds and constantly reflecting on His character. Walking in faith, walking in light, and walking by the Spirit allows us to have a positive attitude in adversities.

The following verses account for walking with God in faith, in light, and by the Spirit:

> 2 Corinthians 5:6-8: *So we are always confident, knowing that while we are at home in the body we are absent from the Lord. For we walk by faith, not by sight. We are confident, yes, well pleased rather to be absent from the body and to be present with the Lord.*

> 1 John 1:7: *But if we walk in the light as He is in the light, we have fellowship with one another, and the blood of Jesus Christ His Son cleanses us from all sin.*

> Galatians 5:16: *I say then: Walk in the Spirit, and you shall not fulfill the lust of the flesh.*

> Galatians 5:25: *If we live in the Spirit, let us also walk in the Spirit.*

We can only fully appreciate all that Jesus has done for us when we see us as He sees us. As we walk in faith, we should be confident that God is always with us, watching over us. Psalm 121:7-8 says, *"The LORD keeps you from all harm and watches over your life. The LORD keeps watch over you as you come and go, both now and forever."* As we walk in light, God's truth and holiness are reflected. Walking by the Spirit is to live not for ourselves but for God, as we become totally dependent upon Him.

## PERSONAL REFLECTION

If you are rightly related to Jesus, then you will seek to align your perspectives with that of God. You will also seek to find His purpose in your life. Reflect on how you can honestly and truly say that your life perspectives are in alignment with that of God by answering these questions:

1. Have you given yourself some time to think and rethink about what you like about yourself and your life? What about what you don't like?

2. Have you examined how you feel about things that are happening, and not happening, to you?

3. Are there areas in your life where you need help, big or small?

4. Are these wants and likes in alignment with God's will for you?

5. Do you give thought to what your purpose in life is?

If there are concerns in some of these areas, I invite you to pray this prayer:

*Heavenly Father, I come before You to present these issues in my life: _____ (mention them). I admit that I may have been deceiving myself in these issues. Please forgive me and help me discern my own life. Help me to understand that only Your love can help to see me through without guilt, shame, condemnation, or fear. I want to be rightly related to You so I can be unleashed from bondage. Provide me with Your Spirit of wisdom and revelation to know You more and Your purpose for my life. I trust You to direct me and guide me to the right path. Amen.*

## Our Relationship to Others

As members of God's family, He is the Father, and we are His children. Likewise, God also gave us our human families here on earth. Although God has made every human being a unique person, we also have many things in common, like our physical shape, abilities, thoughts, and emotions. As human beings, we all have the natural desire to seek God. Unfortunately, many people have a substitute "god" to which they devote their lives. Indeed, God loves us so much that He gave us human choices—free will. There are only two choices or ways of life: we can choose to follow right or wrong, good or evil, heaven or hell. Because of this, conflicts in the family and with others do exist. How well do you know the relationship with your family and others, and what's the best way to deal with it?

Our relationships with parents, spouses, and children are important, no matter how dysfunctional they might be. Many resources are available to help make a healthy relationship better, but is there easy access to these resources? This can be a challenge for any family. Even though we want help, where do we truly find help? With both Christian and non-Christian counselors out there, we're still not 100 percent guaranteed that our needs will be met. However, God is always available and within our reach. Revelation 3:20 says, *"Behold, I stand at the door and knock. If anyone hears My voice and opens the door, I will come in to him and dine with him, and he with Me."*

In our immediate circle of family, where some members are saved but others are not, this could create a big problem. Most often, family members just don't discuss the issue in order to avoid more conflict. There can also be conflict in a family where they were all Christians at one time, but some follow a path in a different direction. This can create chaos and heavy burdens on the family members. But as members of the family of God, all we can do is to pray for them and love them as we lift our concerns to God. In this book, however, my focus is on our relationship with others and examining for ourselves how we can relate to them as we seek maturity in our spiritual growth. God will give guidance and direction as we become rightly related to Him. Our central focus is for God to be the center of our lives.

It's a struggle to have an unsaved member of the family. It's also a struggle if the person is saved but went back to his or her old ways. I remember one day when my daughter shared with me how sad it would be for her not to see her sister in heaven. All I could say was that we needed to keep praying for her no matter how long it took. Although it hurts, you still love that person, and there's nothing that can separate you from him or her, just like what Jesus did for us.

I also remember one of my dearest friends once said to me that she regretted that her son failed to finish school. She even went for her graduate degree just to prove to him that education is very important. She was upset by the fact that her son disobeyed her, but I told her to just keep praying for him. As a mother, it is easy to put the blame onto ourselves. I did for many years until I surrendered my life to God. Henceforth, it has become a way of life for me to pray often and together with my husband; we always pray for our family, friends, and others.

My prayer is for the promise of God to be with everyone who loves and serves Him. Hebrews 13:5 says, *"Let your conduct be without covetousness; be content with such things as you have. For He Himself has said, 'I will never leave you nor forsake you.'"* The Lord never ceases to love and protect us no matter what differences we have between our families or others. God always deals with us just as we are. Being able to identify and understand our differences as we allow God to control our lives will create in us spiritual growth. We must walk with God, call upon Him, and trust in His ways, not ours. For many, if not most of us, family relationships are still a big work in progress, and allowing God to intervene in all areas of our relationships is very much needed.

Another day-to-day struggle for many is becoming focused on doing things outside of family needs. Mothers are sometimes known to be multitaskers, and fathers are sometimes regarded as being married to their jobs. Those are a lot of important priorities that are not being addressed in the family. We want the best for our family, but if the best is not centered around God, then we certainly fail. Or better yet, because things are not what we want or beyond our control, then we become easily frustrated and begin to falter. This is a big test of our faith in God. We need to be rooted to the very foundation of our faith. Knowing God and walking with God reinforces our family relationships as it amplifies our personal relationship with Him. Being rightfully related to God as we continually walk in faith with Him will bring us to a higher level of intimacy with God, thus allowing Him to use us to glorify Him.

Congratulations, we just moved a step forward in our Christian journey. We have discovered basic foundational knowledge and understanding about our relationship with God, ourselves, and others. Establishing our relationship with God will create in us a deeper longing for His presence. Sometimes we can clearly picture in our minds and hearts what to expect for the future as we begin to dream for God, ourselves, and others. The next step will explain why we have to go through this process to dream the dream of a Christian life.

# Are We Dreamers?

The purpose of this chapter is to encourage us to dream a dream for God, for ourselves, and for others. This is *Step Two* in our journey with God. Reliving Joseph's story in the Bible as a dreamer for God will help us realize how we can see all of our extraordinary dreams, hopes, and desires become a reality. Indeed, Joseph acknowledged and gave full credit to God for the interpretations of dreams, and this is what we must do. God used a dream to reveal prophecy. In modern times, dreams and visions can mean the same thing, so much so that we should become visionaries as we create our passion for Christian living. Are we dreamers for God, ourselves, and others? We will then explore what it means to be a dreamer in our daily walk with Jesus.

## Dreamer for God

According to Andrew Ray,

The Bible defines a dream in Job 33:15, 'In a dream, in a vision of the night, when deep sleep falls on people as they slumber in their beds.' The Bible says several things in this one verse. First of all, a dream is a vision of the night. The verse also teaches that a dream occurs when deep sleep falls upon men. According to the Bible, a vision is something that occurs when a man is awake, while a dream is something that occurs when a man is asleep.[1]

Job 33:15 also reminds us that God does speak to us in many ways, such as through our dreams and visions, in order to direct our paths and protect us from evil ways. If our dreams seem to be scary, then we should become more alert to what is going on around us. On the other hand, if our dreams seem to make us happy or give us hope, then we should meditate on them.

Andrew Ray talks about the common purposes for dreams:

1. There were times when God used a dream to give a warning. Matthew 2:12 says, *"And having been warned in a dream not to go back to Herod, they returned to their country by another route."* The Lord appeared to the wise men here for the purpose of warning them not to return to Herod but to go back home another way.

2. There were times when God used a dream to reveal prophecy. Joseph was a man subject to dreams and the interpretations of dreams. In Genesis 37, Joseph dreamed a dream about his brethren bowing down to him.

3. There were times when God used a dream to encourage. In Judges 7, we find the Lord thinning out the army of Gideon before he goes to battle

1. Andrew Ray, Learning the Bible, "What Does the Bible Say about Dreams?" http://www.learnthebible.org/what-does-the-bible-say-about-dreams.html.

with the vast army of Midian. There was an interpretation of a dream that the army of Gideon was going to defeat the Midianites. Immediately upon hearing this dream, Gideon was strengthened, and he worshipped God.

Today we associate dreams with our visions. Very often we say, "My dream is to become a. . . ." By saying this, we really mean what we hope to be or have in the future that is accompanied by our courage and passion to pursue it. When we were young, our parents used to ask about our dreams, but truly they were asking what we were hoping to become, or simply our vision in life. Actually, many young people's dreams are nothing but prosperity and pleasure. As we grow older, we tend to be more realistic with our dreams. When we mature in our spiritual walk with God, our dreams become more truthful, and we're more determined to achieve them. I posed the question, *Are we dreamers for God?* Many Christians may not have ever considered this question. But dreamers for God, to me, relates to our obedience and faithfulness to His commands. God is perfect in every way, so our vision for Him is how we live our lives to be worthy as children of God.

At a very young age, I had this dream/vision of serving God. But quickly it faded away for a long period of time until I accepted Jesus as my Lord and Savior. Then I began to recapture my dream for God. Now it's almost my everyday prayer of envisioning how to live my life for the purpose of the kingdom. I would be lost without God in my life.

Genesis 37:5-11 is about Joseph's dreams of greatness. Reliving his life and his dreams will help us realize how we can see all of our extraordinary dreams, hopes, and desires become a reality.

*Now Joseph had a dream, and he told it to his brothers; and they hated him even more. So he said to them, "Please hear this dream which I have dreamed: There we were, binding sheaves in the field. Then behold, my sheaf arose and also stood upright; and indeed your sheaves stood all around and bowed down to my sheaf." And his brothers said to him, "Shall you indeed reign over us? Or shall you indeed have dominion over us?" So they hated him even more for his dreams and for his words. Then he dreamed still another dream and told it to his brothers, and said, "Look, I have dreamed another dream. And this time, the sun, the moon, and the eleven stars bowed down to me." So he told it to his father and his brothers; and his father rebuked him and said to him, "What is this dream that you have dreamed? Shall your mother and I and your brothers indeed come to bow down to the earth before you?" And his brothers envied him, but his father kept the matter in mind.*

These prophetic dreams of Joseph show God's sovereign purpose in Joseph's life. God had already set joy before Joseph, even at a young age, and so it is with us Christians. God has ways of preparing us beforehand for the trials we cannot foresee. In this case, it appeared to Joseph in his dreams. When he shared these dreams with his brothers, they immediately rejected any meaning of his dreams; instead, they hated him all the more, and they became jealous of him. Not everyone we share our dreams with will be happy about it. But Jacob, Joseph's father, was not really surprised, considering that Joseph was his favorite among his children and the firstborn right had already been given to him. Therefore, he continued to ponder the meaning of Joseph's dreams.

Jacob kept Joseph's dreams in his heart, only to realize later the greatness of these dreams. Joseph became the assistant to the pharaoh after he was sold by his brother to the Egyptians, who would then save them from hunger during the famine in the land. Joseph never gave up his dreams, and neither should we. Joseph acknowledged and gave full credit to God for the interpretations of dreams, and this is what we must do.

> *D—Dream the dreams that come from God*
> *R—Reminding us of His great plans and love*
> *E—Eternal glory is waiting for us up above*
> *A—Almighty Father in heaven shall be our guide*
> *M—May He provide our dreams of greatness*

I truly believe that through our dreams and visions, God will make known His great plans for us. God is a great dreamer, and He has a dream for us, whether we understand Him or not. Our Father in heaven knows us very well and has already prepared us for any unforeseen events.

*"Now all glory to God, who is able, through his mighty power at work within us, to accomplish infinitely more than we might ask or think"* (Eph 3:20 NLT). This Scripture refers to the unlimited power of God that works in us, which is far beyond our comprehension. We need to make sure that we are always in agreement with God's conditions: (1) that Christ may dwell in our hearts through faith and that we are rooted and grounded in His love; (2) that we may be filled with all the fullness of God through the love of Christ; and (3) that we would be granted according to His riches, glory, and strength through the Holy Spirit. Do not be shaken by your own misguided and limited human understanding or the improbabilities because God is real. Isaiah 40:31 says, *"But those who trust in the LORD will find new strength. They will soar high on wings like eagles. They will run and not grow weary. They will walk and not faint."* Remember, it's only through faith that we can put our complete trust and confidence in God and His Word.

As we grow older, we tend to keep our dreams to ourselves. But our dreams and visions must be centered on God. Biblically speaking, dreams and visions are direct revelations from God. It is my conviction that if we have dreams and visions, they should be in alignment with God and in agreement with His commands and promises. God truly and divinely communicates to us through our dreams and visions as reflected by our character. So, having said that, are we dreamers for God? Do we hope to achieve God's purpose for our lives through His revelation in our dreams and visions? The time from conception to manifestation of a dream may be a long time; it's a process. There is also a chance it may never happen. My advice is not to give up. With God in control, the result is always what is best for us.

I went to Catholic school and graduated from a Catholic university; it was there where I dreamt of becoming a nun. At that time, that was the only way I could imagine myself serving God and becoming closer to Him. I kept this dream to myself. As I grew up, my priorities changed, just like with any teenager. Although I always seemed to dream about being a nun. I completely lost touch of this dream for God when I got married because I knew that nuns can't get married. After hitting rock bottom in my marriage, I was in great despair, so I cried out to God for help. Just then, I landed into Jesus' arms and found comfort and peace. At that moment, I realized I had to reclaim my long-lost dream. This was the beginning of a newfound passion to serve God. As I began to grow in my relationship with God, I was convinced that this was the realization and manifestation of my dreams. All along, this dream had been interwoven into every fiber of my life as I yearned for God's presence every day.

Therefore, being a dreamer for God is an absolute and godly call of obedience and faithfulness to Him. Through His guidance, He will direct us to a much better position. The truth is, God will pave the way for our dreams to happen; He is in control of all situations, bad or good. We need to look beyond adversity and insecurity to see God's greater purpose. He has already prepared us beforehand for the trials we can't foresee. Trust God for our dreams. *"God is faithful, by whom you were called into the fellowship of His Son, Jesus Christ our Lord"* (1 Cor 1:9).

# Dreamer for Ourselves

I believe that I became a writer because of God's divine plan for my life. My personal experience of the power of God's Word truly penetrated into my soul as He conveyed every essence of His message. It was indeed a dream come true for me. I would like to think that my writing is God's message to me. I believe it became possible out of obedience and faithfulness to study His Word, understand the truth, and apply the message. As I continue to mature in my walk with Him, I gain wisdom each day as I seek His holy presence. I have learned to pray to God more than ever before.

I also believe that God continually indwells in me the passion to write more. I will never get tired dreaming of all the good things God has put into my heart. Nevertheless, I trust that my physical ailment, Ossification of the Posterior Longitudinal Ligaments (OPLL), will not deter any of these dreams. I sincerely hope and pray that all of God's Word, every testimony, and every prayer presented in this book will continue to minister deeply into the heart of every reader.

The more I seek God in my life, the more I envision the things I want to do to serve Him. Thus I learned to pray for, and about, everything. I need God's confirmation and blessing. I mentioned before that our dreams should be for God. This must be our priority in order for God to redirect our dreams to honoring and glorifying Him. We will most definitely fail or fall if we hold our dreams to ourselves without inviting God to intervene. Part of the process is that we need to listen to God because He speaks to us and knows us intimately. Psalm 139 reveals God's perfect knowledge of our being.

*Dear God, nothing is hidden from You*
*You have searched me and known me*
*From my lying down until my rising up*
*You understand my thoughts*
*You comprehend my path, and*
*You are acquainted with all my ways.*

*Your knowledge is too wonderful for me*
*It is high, I cannot attain it*
*Where can I go from Your Spirit?*
*Where can I flee from Your presence?*
*If I ascend into heaven, You are there*
*If the darkness falls on me, You hold me*

*Indeed, the darkness shall not hide from You*
*But the night shines as the day*
*The darkness and the light are both alike to You.*

*Dear God, nothing is hidden from You*
*For You formed my inward parts and*
*You covered me in my mother's womb*

*I will praise you, for I am fearfully and wonderfully made*
*Marvelous are your works,*
*And that my souls knows very well*

*Search me, O God, and know my heart*
*Try me and know my anxieties and*
*See if there's any wicked way in me*
*And lead me in the way everlasting.*
*Amen.*[2]

---

2. Author's paraphrase.

According to John C. Maxwell, "Dreams are conceived long before they are achieved. The period of time between the birth of a dream and its realization is always a process. Such a period is filled with doubts, adversity, changes, and surprises. During the process, you will experience good days and bad days. And frequently you will be faced with dilemma: Do you give-up or go on?"[3] I say, never give up on your dreams. Just remember that roadblocks do occur, but giving up on your dream is not an option. Instead, strive to align those dreams with God's will. This will help us to become focused on God, and then the passion will come alive as it speaks to our inner being. We may one day abandon our dreams or visions, but God always allows us to recapture them. This has happened to me.

While I was having doubts about keeping up and sorting out things to mend my troubled relationship, I thought about just dropping everything, ending the relationship, and filing for divorce. I was going to leave everything to my husband, including the custody of the children. Then I would just join the mission field helping poor people. I had mentioned this plan to my husband many times before. But God did not allow it to happen because He had better plans for me. He enabled me to recapture the once long-lost dream of serving Him—but in a different way. It came at the right moment and in the right way; it was His way, not mine. I had to go through a series of trials and tribulations before I could attest to the truth about God's plan, His love, and His confirmation.

Hebrews 10:22 says, *"Let us draw near to God."* We have to be rightly related to Him because intimacy with God is the purpose of our lives. This is the reason He created us— to have an intimate relationship with Him. Yes, we should believe in Him and obey Him, but we should also love Him,

---

3. John C. Maxwell, *Running with the Giants* (Nashville: Faith-Words, 2002), 28.

align our lives with Him, and build an intimate relationship with Him.

God knows what is going on in our lives and how we live our lives. Therefore, our dreams are always made known to Him. Romans 8:29-30 says, *"For whom He foreknew, He also predestined to be conformed to the image of His Son, that He might be the firstborn among many brethren. Moreover whom He predestined, these He also called; whom He called, these He also justified; and whom He justified, these He also glorified."* The crown of glory belongs to God. We must then conform to His image and likeness just as we should have constant dependence on Him and be in subjection to Him. And as we walk by faith and in hope for the Lord, He continually stays with us, refines us, sustains us, and reshapes us in the way he wants us to be. This is a mighty encouragement to our faith and hope—for, as for God, His way, His result, and His work are perfect. Just because things don't go as planned, there's no reason to give up. Therefore, as we dream the dream that was laid down before us by God, we patiently wait upon Him to be worthy of His calling.

## Dreamer for Others

Romans 13:8-9 says, *"Owe no one anything except to love one another, for he who loves another has fulfilled the law. For the commandments,* 'You shall not commit adultery, You shall not murder, You shall not steal, You shall not bear false witness, *You shall not covet, and if there is any other commandment, are all summed up in this saying, namely, You shall love your neighbor as yourself."* These Scriptures include all the laws of God about our relationship to others. Our love for others can only be achieved when we do things for their best interest. Then we can become dreamers for them.

As we continue dreaming for God, it becomes a natural reaction to also dream for others. This is part of our human nature as true believers. Loving God to loving others is a natural progression. Parents, for instance, always have dreams for their children. In the beginning, oftentimes we become so excited that we claim ownership to the dream, only to realize later on it's not ours. Therefore, ask God to provide you with a spirit of wisdom and revelation for these dreams to work for you as well as others. Remember Joseph said that his interpretation of dreams came from God. Every fabric of our being, every cell in our body, and every one of our thoughts belongs to God. Don't give up; instead, bring your dreams to God. Psalm 37:4 says, *"Delight yourself also in the LORD, And He shall give you the desires of your heart."*

Sometimes our families are not very supportive of our dreams. But if they come from God, these dreams will hold us in bad times and in good times. When I left my other job to become a financial advisor, it was liberating. Reaching out and being able to minister to people in the workplace became possible. I leveraged my access to a lot of people in this industry to do my counsel, both financial and spiritual. Determined to counsel my clients in their life planning carried me to a higher level of understanding of life. I became more compassionate to people, which later led me to bring every concern and every problem before God for wisdom. I became more prayerful. God sustained me and strengthened me every step of the way. My dream to help other people became more real as I put God at the forefront of my counsel. *"Looking unto Jesus, the author and finisher of our faith, who for the joy that was set before Him endured the cross, despising the shame, and has sat down at the right hand of the throne of God"* (Heb 12:2). Fixing our eyes unto Jesus for our faith and salvation as He perseveres to accomplish God's will for us will draw us closer to God. And His power that works in us will help us to realize how we can see all of our extraordinary dreams, hopes, and desires become a reality.

John C. Maxwell's book *Running with the Giants* provides words of encouragement relative to Joseph who never gave up his dreams, despite all the trouble he went through with his brothers.

God is always with you even in trials and temptations.

Develop yourself during the down times. When you suffer injustice or hard times, complaining doesn't do you any good. When people knock you down, the best thing you can do is allow it to make you better. Each time you find yourself in trouble, try to learn something new.

Realize that self-promotion can never replace divine promotion. Remember that your successes came from God and you must give God the credit.

When the dream is realized, it is sweeter than you can ever imagine. When the dream is God-given, its fulfillment is worth the wait and the realization will far exceed your expectation.[4]

The book also says, "God has in mind for us more than we can imagine. He is the giver of every good and perfect gift, and the fulfiller of every dream He gives."

Needless to say, our dreams for God, for ourselves, and for others should all be for the benefit of God's heavenly kingdom. Therefore, we should strive to become good contributors in society and the world as God originally and purposely intended for man, as stated in Genesis 1:27-28: *"So God created mankind in his own image, in the image of God he created them; male and female he created them. God blessed*

---

4. John C. Maxwell, *Running with the Giants* (Nashville: Faith-Words, 2002).

*them and said to them, 'Be fruitful and increase in number; fill the earth and subdue it. Rule over the fish in the sea and the birds in the sky and over every living creature that moves on the ground.'"* God has brought us into His worldwide family of people who love Him.

God wants every Christian to take part in His work in the world; thus we are called to be His servants. Compelled by Jesus' love—that is so great that He died for our sins—we should follow Him and be committed to letting Him work in our lives. In doing so, we will become concerned for others who have physical and spiritual needs and begin to be dreamers for these people. God wants us to be sensitive to their needs and do what we can to help. We can do so many things as God's servants, so we need to pray for direction, guidance, and discernment.

If we rely entirely on God's guidance, His direction, His provision, and His power given to us by His Holy Spirit, He will make all things possible. Our faithfulness and obedience to God to serve others is our Christian act of faith. If we are dreamers for others as we take part in God's work and do it His way, God will pave the way for us as much as He also prepares those who receive the message. This was exactly what happened with the mission I had in the Philippines. It started with my dream to help people in the Philippines. At first, I did not have any clue of what kind of help or services I should be bringing to these people. But I prayed to God for guidance and direction, and it was all revealed to me.

Becoming a dreamer for God, for myself, and for others unlocked yet another purposeful and godly mission. Actually, it is not very unusual for an immigrant like me to dream of going back to their home country to help the needy. This was also *my* dream. It was in the early part of October 2012 when I was asked to speak at my graduation, and I prayed to God about what to say. After I prepared my speech, I felt like there was something missing that needed to be addressed. It was at the last minute that I had to make a few changes. I had to proclaim the missionary project that I planned on doing in the Philippines. Perhaps it was God's way of confirming the event. Although I didn't know what that mission was going to be, all I could remember was praying fervently to God this prayer:

*Dear heavenly Father, I thank You for this time that I am now about to graduate, and thank You for making it all happen. I would never be in this position if not for Your provisions and guidance. In spite of all the challenges and difficulties that I had to go through, You sustained me physically, emotionally, financially, and spiritually. There were times in the middle of my studies when my mind went blank and I thought,* Why am I doing this? *Often I asked You, Father, "Could this be a part of Your plan for me?" Many more questions came to my mind, but it didn't matter any longer because I felt like every time I sat down to start my studies, You were there by my side.*

*By then I realized that my studies were not all about me, but it was all about You. So I could get closer to You each day that I opened and read Your Word. I was therefore determined to graduate because You gave me all the strength, financially and physically, I needed each day. The countless hours I spent studying never bothered me. Again, because it was You, Father, who I was getting to know, and it was You, Father, to whom I was giving the honor and glory. Indeed, You gave me all that I needed in life. You taught me the best lesson in life, and that is Your Son's (Jesus') life, His teachings, and His examples. Emulating Jesus as the perfect leadership role model gave me a purposeful life.*

*As I am about to finish my studies, Lord, why am I feeling sad? I know I will no longer spend the same hours as I used to studying Your Word. Father, please reveal to me what this is all about and what I need to do. I am afraid I will be in control of my life again instead of You, so please provide me with wisdom and bring purpose to my life. This I pray in Jesus' wonderful name. Amen.*

October 8, 2012, was my graduation day at the Master's International School of Divinity. I was graduating with a doctorate in biblical studies, specializing in biblical leadership. It was a leap of faith for me to be able to pursue this study. The school recognized where I was coming from and the challenges I had to go through, so I was awarded The Conquerors Award, and on the plaque was written, "In recognition of her exceptional overcoming spirit in the completion of her degree." And Romans 8:35-39 was quoted: *"No, in all these we are more than conquerors through Him who loved us."* Praise His holy name, God truly helped me conquer all my doubts and challenges and taught me how to deal with my health problems as I made myself able, willing, and ready to do His will and submit to His purpose.

Coming home after graduation, I spent hours searching and praying for people from the Philippines with whom I could connect to help implement my project. Although there was no specific project yet, I started calling people. It was toward the beginning of November when I called an organization called Eyecarewecare Foundation to see if I could sponsor their January 2012 event to bring vision care to my former hometown. Indeed, God made it happen, and He provided me with all that I needed. Every detail of my dream became real when I arrived in the Philippines to do the missionary and medical/vision care project. Actually, preparation for the mission could have taken up to a year, but

God made it all happen in just over two months, from the planning stage to the financial resources, implementation, and beneficiaries. God is great!

To over 1,560 indigent people, we provided free eye exams, free prescription eyeglasses, and free surgery for cataracts, pterygium, and glaucoma. The highlight to all of this was the ministry mission where we shared the gospel and the Word of God with over two thousand people. The missionary project was simultaneously done with the eye care/medical project. It reminded me of how Jesus healed the sick at the same time that He was teaching wisdom to the multitude. My mission brought hope for the people both physically and spiritually, making known to them the love and greatness of the Lord.

I could certainly assure you that what happened and how it happened was a great affirmation of our living and loving God. Many manifestations of God's great power was working in all of us who were part of the mission. Only our complete trust and confidence in God made it all happen. Therefore, we bring honor and glory to God's wonderful work in us who greatly love Him. Moreover, as we dream the dream for God, for ourselves, and for others, we exalt His name, uphold His promises, and yield to His path. In the end, we will give a solemn declaration that the so-called mysteries are no longer mysteries, and the miracles are no longer miracles, but these are all true, and Jesus' plan is for real.

This mission started from a dream, and, without any doubt, God orchestrated it all. Not only did it help many people be able to see clearly with their physical eyes, but it also allowed them to open their spiritual eyes and hearts to see the truth about Jesus through the ministry. I encourage everyone to be a dreamer for God, to seek His guidance, to follow His direction, and to trust Him completely. This is what makes the world a better place to live. Creating a vision or dreaming a dream for God, for ourselves, and for others is definitely part of the process to make a difference in the Christian life.

## STEP THREE

# Can We Make a Difference?

T he purpose of this chapter is to prepare and encourage us to step out from our comfort zone and begin to fully embrace a new realm of Christian life, thus allowing God to use us for His purpose to make a difference for Him, for ourselves, and in the lives of others. This is Step Three in our journey with God.

Be reminded that the way we live our lives is our representation of God, and if we are obedient to God's truth and faithful to His command, we are glorifying God and making a difference for Him. Queen Esther was a great example of someone who was willing to risk her life just to make a difference for God and for her people. Seeking God to partner with us in our journey can make a great difference for God because we're giving Him control of all situations. Therefore, we must always remember that God has a place for all of us, no matter who we are and no matter what situation we are in. All we can do is trust that He will use us in many ways. Even if you feel out of place, to God you will always have a place in Him.

In Genesis, Noah's obedience and faithfulness to God is something that we want to emulate. When God ordered him to build an ark, he believed in Him, and God spared his life. God always searches our hearts, and He knows when to bring judgments to our faithlessness. Are you striving to make a difference? If so, reflect on it and ask for God's discernment and manifestation into your life as you strive to make a difference as a Christian.

# Making a Difference for God

God gave us life of priceless value for His great purpose. He also made us perfect for that great purpose in order to accomplish it. Therefore, by honoring God and His sovereign works, we are already making a difference for God. Matthew 5:14-16 says, *"You are the light of the world. A city that is set on a hill cannot be hidden. Nor do they light a lamp and put it under a basket, but on a lampstand, and it gives light to all who are in the house. Let your light so shine before men, that they may see your good works and glorify your Father in heaven."* These Scriptures say that we are the light of the world, but it is our choice to hide it or let our light shine before others so they may see God's sovereign works in us. As Christians, we should let our light shine because we become the reflection of God to others.

In the same manner, people will see God's divine character through us. We should make sure that our words, actions, and deeds point people to God, the author of our life and the ultimate source of our light. Letting our light shine before men allows them to see our good works that will magnify God's grace and power. Light has to do with the way we live, which means living our lives in the light is being open and honest with people. Thus far, the way we conduct our lives openly and honestly and the way we lead godly lives to those around us will bring glory to God. That being said, we are making a great difference to God by living our lives believing God's truth and obeying God's command.

Are we choosing to let our light shine before others? If not, why? Being overwhelmed sometimes is a part of the process that we go through each day as we walk by faith with God, but it's also a significant facet to our spiritual growth. With our faith being incessantly tested, we must be on guard for our actions, words, thoughts, and deeds so we will not falter. Oftentimes, we don't seem to be thinking or doing all the right things for God, or we may even be feeling that we are not doing enough to fulfill His will. I have been convicted many times on this, but the good thing about being a true believer is that we have direct access to God to ask for His mercy and forgiveness. Learning from our mistakes is always a part of the process, so we can grow more in our spiritual walk with God. But we have to be obedient and faithful to God at all times. Being spiritually entwined in our personal relationship with the Lord will set forth our desire to make a difference for God, as it creates in us a pure heart.

With the understanding that God created man as His unique masterpiece, we are already predestined for that unique purpose. And as we continue to ask God to manifest into our lives, and as we seek to align our day-to-day activities with Him, our unique calling will be made known to us. Indeed, through our obedience to God's call, we are already making a difference for God. Isaiah 6:8 says, *"Also I heard the voice of the Lord, saying: 'Whom shall I send, And who will go for Us?' Then I said, 'Here am I! Send me.'"* The call of God is not for the special few. Many are called, but only few prove themselves to be the chosen ones. All Christians are called to share the gospel, but it is a challenge for many Christians to follow this great command of God. Unfortunately, many people have no ear for anything but themselves, so they cannot hear God's call. But I truly believe that sharing the gospel can be done anywhere at any time by simply doing your day-to-day activities—for example, meeting or talking to people who are in desperate need of a friend or visiting a friend or a neighbor who is sick or has problems. It doesn't have to happen in just one meeting; it could be a series of meetings or conversations. Always pray for God to intervene in these divine appointments. Remember to pray for discernment.

> The book of Esther teaches us how we can make a difference for God. The story of Queen Esther is a great example of someone who was willing to risk her life just to make a difference for God. If there was someone with a strong sense of place and destiny, it was Esther. However, for many of her years, she did not realize that God had a special place for her to serve Him. "For much of my life," she says, "I felt out of place. My parents died when I was very young, and I was adopted by my uncle Mordecai. There were times I felt out of place in his home. As I grew up in a strange country with different customs, again I felt out of place. And being a simple girl, being brought to the king's court made me feel out of place as well."

> Esther lived during a time when the Hebrews had been taken from their homeland and exiled to Persia. She suffered many hardships in her life, but she also received a rare opportunity. When King Ahasuerus of Persia sought a new queen, all the most beautiful young, unmarried women in the land were brought together and prepared to be presented to him. That included Esther, even though she was Jewish—a fact she did not share

with others. To her delight and that of Mordecai, she was chosen by Ahasuerus to be the queen.

It looked as if Esther's life was destined for a happy, storybook ending. But then an official named Haman in the king's court plotted to have all the Jews in the entire kingdom executed—simply because of a grudge he held against Mordecai. When Mordecai discovered the plan, he sought Esther's help. To save their people, Mordecai wanted her to appeal to the king.[5]

This is a very profound story about courage, initiative, and creativity used to save innocent people. When Mordecai sought Queen Esther's help, she was very much troubled about how to reach out to the king. With Haman as an official to the king and Esther, being Jewish just made it even harder. Queen Esther had to be courageous and adamant about saving her people. But with Queen Esther's creative actions and Mordecai's encouragement, God ministered to her.

When Esther realized that God placed her in the palace for a great purpose, she ordered her people to fast and pray for her, and she did the same. She needed the courage, and God gave it to her in order to make a difference for her people. Queen Esther's act of obedience granted her initiative and great courage.

To end her story, her uncle Mordecai's plan, her plan, and God's plan made a happy ending, and it was Haman instead of Mordecai who was executed. We must always be reminded that submitting to God's plan will always result in what is best for us.

---

5. John C. Maxwell, *Running with the Giants* (Nashville: Faith-Words, 2002), 16.

Another Bible story that demonstrates obedience and faithfulness to God is the story of Noah. Please refer to the book of Genesis from chapter 6 to chapter 10.

> *Then the LORD saw that the wickedness of man was great in the earth, and that every intent of the thoughts of his heart was only evil continually. And the LORD was sorry that He had made man on the earth, and He was grieved in His heart. So the LORD said, "I will destroy man whom I have created from the face of the earth, both man and beast, creeping thing and birds of the air, for I am sorry that I have made them." But Noah found grace in the eyes of the LORD. This is the genealogy of Noah. Noah was a just man, perfect in his generations. Noah walked with God. And Noah begot three sons: Shem, Ham, and Japheth. The earth also was corrupt before God, and the earth was filled with violence. So God looked upon the earth, and indeed it was corrupt; for all flesh had corrupted their way on the earth. And God said to Noah, "The end of all flesh has come before Me, for the earth is filled with violence through them; and behold, I will destroy them with the earth. Make yourself an ark of gopherwood; make rooms in the ark, and cover it inside and outside with pitch."* (Gn 6:5-14)

First, we have to know that Genesis 6:1-5 displays the wickedness of men and the account of their sins, from the lust of the flesh, power, and disobedience to God. Because of their wickedness, Genesis 6:5-14 tell us that God was grieved in His heart, and His patience ran out. Our sin-sorrowed God, who is holy and without blemish, wanted to bring judgment to humanity. But Noah found grace in the eyes of God. Noah's life was spared because of his good works, and he believed in God as Creator. He therefore humbled himself and became obedient to God's will. So when Noah was ordered by God to build an ark, he did. Noah did exactly what God told him to do. This is a story of one man who made a difference for God. Noah's obedience and faithfulness to God is something that we want to emulate so we too can make a great difference for God.

Second Chronicles 16:9 says, *"For the eyes of the LORD run to and fro throughout the whole earth, to show Himself strong on behalf of those whose heart is loyal to Him. In this you have done foolishly; therefore from now on you shall have wars."* God also knows when He can use us to make a difference just like what He did to Noah. Therefore, when we become partners with God, and if we stand in the gap for His will to happen, we must be ready because He wants to use us for His kingdom purpose. God always searches our hearts, and He knows when to bring judgment to our faithlessness.

A true Christian life makes a big difference to the Lord. We come into agreement with His sovereign might and power, and we submit to His deity and reverence as we honor, praise, and glorify His name. Although it's natural for us to want to strive to make a difference in our own lives, living our lives in alignment with God will instill in us a great and godly purpose. This brings me to the next level of Step Three.

## Making a Difference as Christians

When God created us, He already preordained our life's purpose. But finding our purpose is a process, and God gave us choices. *"You can enter God's Kingdom only through the narrow gate. The highway to hell is broad, and its gate is wide for the many who choose that way. But the gateway to life is very narrow and the road is difficult, and only a few ever find it"* (Mt 7:13-14 NLT). These Scriptures describe God's call to us (people) to make a decision on which way to follow. When we come to a crossroads in life, we need to decide which way to go. There are two gates, two ways, and two destinations; thus men will be divided into two groups for their choices. One group will follow the worldly way, and the other group will follow the godly way. Jesus' purpose for redemption is for people to enter the narrow gate; this is the way to heaven, and our destination is God's kingdom as we inherit eternal life. As Christians, we must enter the narrow gate by faith, and it's only through Christ that we can enter.

John 14:6 says, *"I am the way, the truth, and the life. No one comes to the Father except through Me."* This represents true salvation in God's way through repentance, submission to Christ as Lord, and a willingness to obey His will and Word. On the other hand, if man chooses to enter the broad gate, this is the way to hell, and their destination is destruction as they receive everlasting punishment. Therefore, as Christians, we must say "no" to the things of the fallen world that will lead us to destruction and say "yes" to Christ who will lead us to eternal life. We must rely on His power rather than our own.

Below are Scriptures from Colossians describing the behavior and character of true Christians—those who have been chosen by God and who answered God's free, powerful, and sovereign grace. Application of this godly behavior and character will confirm our identity with Christ. These Scriptures say that we have been chosen by God, as we are the object of His unconditional love; therefore, through Jesus, we have been forgiven, so we must be willing to forgive others. Through God's Word, the Holy Spirit gives us life that controls every word, thought, and deed. Thus the Holy Spirit intercedes to bring the message from God to fill our lives with His richness and mercy.

*Therefore, as the elect of God, holy and beloved, put on tender mercies, kindness, humility, meekness, longsuffering; bearing with one another, and forgiving one another, if anyone has a complaint against another; even as Christ forgave you, so you also must do. But above all these things put on love, which is the bond of perfection. And let the peace of God rule in your hearts, to which also you were called in one body; and be thankful. Let the word of Christ dwell in you richly in all wisdom, teaching and admonishing one another in psalms and hymns and spiritual songs, singing with grace in your hearts to the Lord. And whatever you do in word or deed, do all in the name of the Lord Jesus, giving thanks to God the Father through Him.* (Col 3:12-17)

When we choose to follow God's way, we are already making a difference to ourselves as Christians. This is the way of self-denial, surrender, and humility. This also accounts for the Golden Rule passage: *"Therefore, whatever you want men to do to you, do also to them, for this is the Law and the Prophets"* (Mt 7:12). How we treat others is determined by how we want them to treat us. Obeying this rule is a reflection of God's love for us. When making a difference in our lives, we always cater to what God wants for us. *"Let no one despise your youth, but be an example to the believers in word, in conduct, in love, in spirit, in faith, in purity"* (1 Tm 4:12). We can portray ourselves as Christians in word, conduct, love, spirit, faith, and in purity. We should speak good things, for it's by our word that we are either justified or condemned. We are personally responsible for our own conduct. We Christians are called to exemplify the same kind of love that Jesus has for us. And as servants of Christ, we are to become faithful in spirit and in truth.

As Christians, we have to be on guard with our daily activities, be conformed to the attributes of true Christians, create godly driven values and purpose, and exemplify personal accountability; otherwise, we could easily be trapped by self-deception. Unfortunately, there may be times that we are enticed by all the nice things around us. We become focused on ourselves. James 3:16 says, *"For where envy and self-seeking exist, confusion and every evil thing are there."* Therefore, when we are drawn to acquiring worldly things out of greed or self-seeking interest, we will be repudiated from the inheritance of eternal life. We simply become good for nothing.

Always remember that we cannot make a meaningful difference unless we are made different ourselves. Philippians 4:13 says, *"I can do all things through Christ who strengthens me."* As believers in Christ, we are to be strong and resist all temptations. God gave us strength to withstand all things. Jesus infuses strength in us during our difficulties. We must live our lives as God commanded because everything we do, how we behave, and how we think and feel will be a reflection of a true Christian.

If we set the bar high for our behavior and attitude, bearing with one another and forgiving one another, we will truly make a difference.

## Making a Difference in the Lives of Others

When we become rightly related to God, there are so many things we can do for Him. In seeking to serve God, we become His workers and followers. We become workers for God's kingdom and faithful followers of Jesus' footsteps. Under the authority of God, we do God's work His way by relying entirely on the power given to us by His Holy Spirit. Therefore, when we are called to share in God's work, we must serve Him in one accord as we worship Him in righteousness and in truth. God equipped us with His Word to never doubt its truth and relevance through our faith. Moreover, He has gifted us with natural abilities, resources, and talents to use for the fulfillment of His plan and the furtherance of His work. This Christian service is an act of our faithfulness and obedience to God.

Philippians 2:3-4 says, *"Let nothing be done through selfish ambition or conceit, but in lowliness of mind let each esteem others better than himself. Let each of you look out not only for his own interests, but also for the interest of others."* Pride or conceit prompts one to have his or her way in pursuit of personal glory, which Jesus so strongly condemns, because it is a transgression against God. Humbleness brings glory to God. Show respect for others' differences. Indeed, we should focus on the good side of a person, recognizing that everyone has something of value. First Thessalonians 5:11 says, *"Therefore, comfort each other and edify one another, just as you are already doing."* This way, we are exemplifying good Christian character of true humility, which is a great representation of Christ's life in us. Henceforth, we can freely do whatever God wants us to do, and our conduct will glorify Him. Remember, we can never make a difference in the lives of others unless we are truthful to God and to ourselves.

The Lord is deeply grieved when Christians turn back from Him and His ways. But the Lord will do what it takes to bring them back on the path of His plan. Thus if we have a personal concern for others, Jesus can use us as an instrument for His ultimate care. We have to be prepared to bring back the erring ones. James 5:19-20 says, *"My dear brothers and sisters, if someone among you wanders away from the truth and is brought back, you can be sure that whoever brings the sinner back will save that person from death and bring about the forgiveness of many sins."* People who apostatize are in grave danger, and they need to be called back to their true faith. So we need to be praying for these people and try to go out of our way to minister to them and show them our genuine concern, compassion, and love. Emulating the example of

Jesus' love is beyond our comfort level, but it is part of our duty as Christians.

Sometimes in the real world, making a difference in the lives of others means material giving or providing humanitarian aid. These are very noble deeds, and surely there are lots of people in need of this type of help. However, we Christians also need to recognize that these people are not just in need of physical sustenance but spiritual as well. Colossians 1:28-29 says, *"Him we preach, warning every man and teaching every man in all wisdom, that we may present every man perfect in Christ Jesus. To this end I also labor, striving according to His working which works in me mightily."*

One Sunday service at my church, one of the pastors talked about these Scriptures, and I liked the way he presented the study by highlighting four major areas. The *first* is about preaching Christ—the true gospel, which is the good news about Jesus and His redemptive suffering for our sins. Through our faith, our true hope is in Him. The *second* is about warning every man—teaching in error is false teaching, which could lead to deception. Jesus said in Matthew 24:4, *"Take heed that no one deceives you."* The *third* is about teaching God's Word—the Bible, which is God's eternal Word that communicates to us about the truth regarding His nature, His command, and His promises. The *fourth* is about working in Christ's sufficiency—our sufficiency is from God. We can never rely on our own strength; we must rely on God's strength in all aspects of our lives. It is therefore very crucial to incorporate all these major areas and take them very seriously in order to accomplish a godly calling in our missionary or ministry work.

Patience, obedience, and complete trust in God are great characteristics of Christians; we can learn these from the way Abraham led his life. When taking part in God's work, it is always His way and in His time, not ours. Although Abraham was impatient when God promised him that he would possess the land of Canaan and would have many descendants, still, he believed in Him. And God gave it all to Abraham. God always gives what He promises, so we have to be patient no matter how long it takes. Abraham and Sarah were promised that they would have a son. Though it seemed impossible because they were both old, they put their complete trust in God's promise. Sarah indeed gave birth to their son, Isaac. And when Abraham was asked by God to sacrifice his only beloved son, he never doubted God. Instead, he was obedient, which was the true test of his trust in God.

The life of Abraham has made a significant impact in our lives as Christians. By emulating Abraham's obedience and complete trust in God, we become true servants of God, and His plans for us become real and significantly influence others' lives.

God truly empowers us with strength and wisdom to prepare us, to energize us, and to sustain us if we use it for His great purpose. This was testified by God during my missionary trip to the Philippines. Just for a matter of second opinion, I visited one of my neurosurgeons for his assessment of my OPLL illness before I took off to travel for my missionary project. He insisted that I not travel because I would be at a high risk of a possible accident during travel. But because I truly believed that it was God who orchestrated the whole missionary project, I put my complete trust in Him. Praise God nothing bad happened, although I have to admit we were so close to having accidents along the way. My health issue never bothered me at all during the mission; thus I was able to fulfill God's purpose and make a difference to thousands of people.

Inherent in making a difference in the lives of others is our relationship to Christ, other believers, and the world. John 15:1-17 discusses the vine and the branches as a metaphor to Christian living. Jesus is the true vine, the Father is the vinedresser, and we are the branches. The vine has two types of branches: one that bears fruits and one that doesn't. The branches that bear fruit are the true believers, and the branches that do not are those who declare and pretend to be believers. Our Father, the vinedresser, will cut off the dead branches in order to give way to the fruit-bearing branches. Then He prunes the fruit-bearing branches so they will bear more fruit. In real life, God removes our impurities, doubts, sins, and hindrances that drain our spiritual life so we can abide in Him.

As true believers, we obey the Lord's commands, and being committed to His Word, we are devoted to His will. Jesus' love was supremely evidenced by His sacrificial death upon the cross. So we are called to exemplify the same kind of love to others. Unfortunately, Satan dominates the evil world system to rebel against God and against those who are God's followers, as attested in John 15:18: *"If the world hates you, you know that it hated Me before it hated you."* But the Holy Spirit will confront the world testifying about Jesus and convict men of sin. Through the conviction of sin and the testimony of the gospel, the Holy Spirit will turn rebellious hearts into desiring Jesus as their Lord and Savior. We, therefore, as true believers, become part of the work of God through faith as we become obedient to share in the furtherance of the gospel to others— an integral part of making a difference in the lives of others.

Making a difference for God as Christians and in the lives of others has a significant impact on how we live our lives as Christians. Let us now look at an in-depth understanding of living our lives to full capacity.

# Are We Living Our Lives to Full Capacity?

T he purpose of this chapter is threefold: first, to encourage us to understand and live the Christian life to its full capacity; second, to remind us about God's great plan for our lives; and third, to become aware that our faith in God always brings reassurance to our safety from destruction as we encounter the storms of life. This is *Step Four* in our journey with God.

If we strive to fulfill His great plan for our lives, then we are in pursuit of godly living amid the storms of life. Please pray this prayer as you begin to explore God's message in this chapter. Ask God to reveal His personal plan for your life, that, in spite of challenges and difficulties, you thrive to live the Christian life to its full capacity.

> *Heavenly Father, I acknowledge that You have a great plan for my life. Please provide me with the*

*spirit of wisdom to know You more each day as You reveal Your great plans to me. Teach me to rely on Your strength and mighty power to overcome the storms of life and to live a godly life as I obey and trust in You. I ask these in Jesus' name. Amen.*

# In Pursuit of Godly Living

Godly living encompasses all aspects of our lives. Although God loves us the way we are, He also preordained us to do His will and to pursue His kingdom purpose. Pursuing a godly life is not easy; sometimes it can be inconvenient to us. Be reminded that when we accepted Jesus as our Lord and Savior, we were given a new position. Our identity is no longer rooted to who we are; now we are rooted to who Jesus is in our life. We should not become complacent any longer to the things we used to love that were not in accordance with the Law of God. Through grace and mercy, we were given a new identity in Christ Jesus who loves us. Therefore, with the supreme power of Christ, we should ask to be filled with knowledge to understand what God wants to do in our lives, to have godly wisdom, and to lead a life pleasing and honoring to Him. We should also ask for God's power to help us withstand difficulties and that we will be filled with joy, giving thanks for our divine inheritance.

Living a life to its fullest capacity requires an intimate relationship with God. This was made available to us through Jesus' redemptive sufferings and death on the cross. Living a Christian life allows us to experience a better outlook and have a better perspective on the things around us as we live for God, with God, and dependent on God. Living for God and believing in faith with God, Christians receive a new quality of life, which includes hope, love, peace, joy, and power and patience to cope with difficulties. Therefore, as we achieve to live life to the fullest, we must constantly seek God's guidance through reading His Word, praying, and fellowshipping with believers. Never stop learning how to live and lead like Jesus; the Lord will continue to minister and manifest His life in us.

In 1 Thessalonians 5:16-22, the basics of Christian living are discussed: *"Rejoice always, pray without ceasing, in everything give thanks; for this is the will of God in Christ Jesus for you. Do not quench the Spirit. Do not despise prophecies. Test all things; hold fast what is good. Abstain from every form of evil."* Paul provided the foundational principles for our spiritual life: have a joyful heart and pray regularly and persistently; giving thanks for everything is God's will for us; believers are under the power of the Holy Spirit, so we must walk in Spirit and in truth; the Scriptures are God's revelations to us to guide and protect us from the evil ones.

In 1 Thessalonians 4:11, Paul gives instruction concerning the disciplines of Christian living: *"That you also aspire to lead a quiet life, to mind your own business, and to work with your own hands, as we commanded you."*

This is what Paul said in 1 Corinthians 1:3-6 concerning spiritual gifts: *"Grace to you and peace from God our Father and the Lord Jesus Christ. I thank my God always concerning you for the grace of God which was given to you by Christ Jesus, that you were enriched in everything by Him in all utterance and all knowledge, even as the testimony of Christ was confirmed in you."* God our Father, through Jesus who redeemed us from our sins, provides believers with all the knowledge needed in order to speak effectively of Him. So we must. This will attest to our obedience and faithfulness to God—to openly and boldly speak about the gospel. It might not be a comfortable thing to do, but it is an important aspect to godly living.

As Christians, we are given spiritual wealth that comes with God's great love, but with it comes great responsibilities. However, God still gives us the ability to choose what to do with our lives. If you pursue godly living, you must stay in alignment with His purpose and your allegiance to His command and deity that surpasses everything.

The following are a few of the verses that depict the essential qualities of godly living:

*"Beloved, I beg you as sojourners and pilgrims, abstain from fleshly lusts which war against the soul"* (1 Pt 2:11). Christians must discipline themselves by avoiding the desire of the fallen world. Hold yourself away from fleshly lusts that will destroy the Christian's joy and peace.

*"And do not be conformed to this world, but be transformed by the renewing of your mind, that you may prove what is that good and acceptable and perfect will of God"* (Rom 12:2). As Christians, our actions should be a reflection of the truth about what is in our hearts. We must resist compromise and pursue the good things that are consistent to godly driven values. In order to live a godly life, Paul urges believers to give control of their lives to God. This is the right thing to do after all the things He has done for us. Renewing your mind is simply changing your thought processes to the things of God and not to the things of this world. This spiritual transformation happens from the inside out, as it will be reflected in the way we live our lives.

*"Therefore, if anyone is in Christ, he is a new creation; old things have passed away; behold, all things have become new"* (2 Cor 5:17). Our security is in Christ as we become rightly related to Him. When we accepted Christ into our lives and asked for His forgiveness, we became clean, our sins were all washed away, and we became a new creation; our old value systems, priorities, and belief systems are gone. Our spiritual perception of everything is all about God, for God, and to God.

*"Do not love the world or the things in the world. If anyone loves the world, the love of the Father is not in him. For all that is in the world—the lust of the flesh, the lust of the eyes, and the pride of life—is not of the Father but is of the world"*

(1 Jn 2:15-16). The world has much to offer, and although it may appear attractive and appealing, do not be deceived by it because its true nature is harmful. To love the world is to disregard the Lord. Things of the world are lust, which refers to a strong desire for evil things, and flesh, which refers to the sinful nature of man. If our eyes are focused on these things, we will be enticed and captivated by them. The pride of life is edifying ourselves, parading what we possess in order to impress others. Indeed, we can never lead a godly life if our hearts are full of pride.

Dr. Charles Stanley says,

> The key to living a godly life is full surrender. That means we must let God have complete control over our lives. The Lord is looking for faithful men and women who will stand up for truth in a world that is increasingly opposed to the gospel. Rather than base your standards on popular opinion, allow Scripture to set your values. Answer the Lord's call to a godly life, and you will never be the same.[6]

Norman Vincent Peale says, "Change your thoughts and everything changes. Your life is determined by the kind of thoughts you habitually think." In order to live a godly life, our actions and reactions should conform to our thoughts. These thoughts must be centered on God's commands, teachings, and examples. Let our thought processes be dominated by godly driven values and lifestyle. According to Peale, life is what your thoughts make it. The kind of thoughts you think determine the exact kind of world in which you live. Peale added, "Change your thoughts and you will change your

6. Dr. Charles Stanley, "A Call to Godly Living," http://www.intouch.org/resources/sermon-outlines/Content.aspx?topic=A_Call_to_Godly_Living_Sermon_Outline

world. Change your thoughts correctly and everything will change into inner peace, happiness, and personal power."[7]

Therefore, what we think today, what we have been thinking long before, and what we think of the future plays a big role in how we live our lives. The changes that occurred in my life during the past six years are a testimony to how I changed my thought processes for the better. As a young girl, I always had the desire to serve God, but it did not really happen until these last six years because I was so preoccupied with the things of the world. But from the moment I accepted Jesus into my life, a lot of changes occurred. Intimacy with the Lord became my priority as I devoted my time to learning about Him. I've since been in constant yearning for His presence and His manifestation in my life. I began to read the Bible a lot, and I prayed a lot—not just for me but for other people. Triggered by my earnest desire to serve God, I discovered avenues to improve my knowledge of Him and my deepest longing to know His purpose for me. All the good things that happened in my life these past six years created more purpose and a true meaning of life. Changing my thoughts for God changed everything for the better, allowing me to serve God and live my life to full capacity.

Godly living is a step-by-step process. Everyone is different; some take baby steps while others take big steps. I would like to share some of the process I went through that continually guided me to godly living.

1. *Understand what being a Christian is.* Being a Christian, we have a close personal relationship with God. We live a life with God in faith, we live a life given by God through our obedience to His commands, and we live a life dependent on God by trusting Him.

7. Norman Vincent Peale, *A Guide to Confident Living* (New York: Touchstone, 2003), 230.

2.  *Choose to become a Christian.* To become a Christian, we accept Jesus as our Lord and Savior. We ask God to forgive us from all of our sins and then start a new way of living.

3.  *Develop intimacy with God.* To become intimate with God, we read God's Word, pray, worship, and fellowship as we reflect on the following:

    *Learning process:* God's commands, promises, and provisions

    *Growing process:* personally and relationally with God and others

    *Discovering process:* God's way, God's purpose, and God's will

    *Application process:* ministry, discipleship, evangelism, etc.

# Finding Life Purpose

Why are we here? What is our life purpose? And how do we know God's purpose for our lives? I believe that these questions cannot be truthfully answered without knowing our Creator, His great love, and His plan for mankind. We do not own our life. As Christians, when we became rightly related to God, we no longer control our lives. We surrender to His will and purpose, which is permanent, truthful, solid, and absolute. I hope the following verses provide guidance, direction, and wisdom to discerning and finding God's purpose.

It says in 1 Corinthians 15:10, *"But by the grace of God I am what I am, and His grace toward me was not in vain; but I labored more abundantly than they all, yet not I, but the grace of God which was with me."* God created us in His image and likeness. He also gave us life of priceless value for His great purpose. Because of sin, we have to bring ourselves into repentance and humility before God. By the grace of God, we are forgiven as we accept Jesus as our personal Redeemer and Lord. Our personal relationship with God will begin to evolve. Thus we learn to understand that we are saved and sanctified by God, submitting ourselves completely to His truth and purpose. When sanctified by God, we allow Him to use us, much like He used Jesus for our salvation.

Deuteronomy 6:5 says, *"You shall love the Lord your God with all your heart, with all your soul, and with all your strength."* Loving God with all our heart, soul, and strength should be our basic aim in life. If we begin to seek great purpose only for ourselves, we create a hindrance for God to use us. God's purpose is always about Him and not about us. Therefore, as Christians, we pray to God to bring clarity into our hearts and minds as we begin to ask for wisdom and discernment.

It says in 1 Corinthians 6:19, *"Or do you not know that your body is the temple of the Holy Spirit who is in you, whom you have from God, and you are not your own?"* Our Christian bodies belong to the Lord, and we are brought into fellowship with Jesus' redemptive sufferings. Therefore, we are called into the fellowship of the gospel and to God Himself. All our abilities and powers should be pointed toward God's purpose and in glorifying Him.

In life, we suffer pain, anguish, turmoil, and fear, and through our heartbreaks, God intervenes and picks us up. We often associate this with our awakening call. It says in 2 Peter 3:9, *"The Lord isn't really being slow about his promise, as some people think. No, he is being patient for your sake. He does not want anyone to be destroyed, but wants everyone to repent."* God's promise is to never leave us nor forsake us—most certainly in our brokenness where He can bring His purpose. Though sometimes we don't feel the connection and don't seem to hear Him in the midst of the storm, God is always with us. Trust in Him and pray for deliverance. This may be the time when He is preparing us for a greater purpose. As we become obedient and faithful, we will be awakened by God's call. Be available and willing to embrace that call.

There may be times when we know that our vision is in line with God's will and purpose. We must be obedient to that call so we can live in the light of that vision. *"For many are called, but few are chosen"* (Mt 22:14). Remember, not everyone is called to preach the gospel, but if we truthfully and passionately believe that we are called to do so, then His purpose will be revealed. Isaiah 6:8 says, *"Then I heard the voice of the Lord saying, 'Whom shall I send? And who will go for us?' And I said, 'Here am I. Send me!'"* And if we agree with God's purpose, then He will bring into harmony every aspect of your life.

Because we are uniquely created, we each have a unique calling. Through this uniqueness, God can use us for different purposes.

When we have realized our calling, we become servants to God's own purpose. Although we are created to glorify God and enjoy Him forever, sin came into the human race. But by God's grace, we were rectified. I believe God predestined me for missionary work, so I make sure that my missionary work reflects a servant's leadership. Therefore, God will be edified and glorified. We must not be confused with our own personal intentions when we are called to do God's work; otherwise, we become subjected to our own personal interests.

Only God knows why we are here, but I truly believe we are here for a purpose. We must trust God and be in communion with Him because He surely knows what's best for us. We can begin by understanding God's heart for us and the fullness of God in our lives. As we relate them to our personal lives and the things we want to do, then God will help position us for great use. This positioning may not be the exact place God wants us to end up, but it's a stepping stone. When we align ourselves with God, it influences the kingdom. When we become passionate about our purpose and continually draw our strength from His Word, then finding God's purpose is a natural progression. Running well the race of faith will draw us closer to that purpose. *"Fight the good fight of faith, lay hold on eternal life, to which you were also called and have confessed the good confession in the presence of many witnesses"* (1 Tm 6:12).

Instead of dwelling on the questions, *Why we are here?* or *What is the purpose of life?*— maybe we should focus on the things we do best or have the most of: time, talents, treasures, abilities. Then use them for the purpose of edifying and glorifying the Lord. Be reminded that we are created in His image and likeness, and to question God for what you view as bad things—miseries, trials, tribulations, physical appearance—is an insult to our Creator. Just remember that God is always with us no matter what conditions our lives are in. God can use us fully if we make ourselves able, willing, and ready to do His will. Have faith in God and remain obedient to Him. We must put our trust in God's hand because He has already preordained our purpose both here on earth and in heaven.

*Prayer*

*Heavenly Father, please allow us to look beyond adversities to see Your greater purpose in us. Take control of our lives and empower us with the things that promote love, joy, peace, and happiness. Provide us with knowledge and understanding to carry out the purpose for which You have called us. Bring wisdom and discernment to our hearts as we seek to take part in Your work here on earth as it is in heaven. Amen.*

My passion for living had a great impact on me, forming my deepest longing to serve God. This long and wearisome process became a reality, and I would like to share this part of my story. It was never on my list of things to do or in my dreams to be serving God in this capacity. Everything that happened in my life these past six years was unbelievable to me. As I glance back to six years earlier, it was difficult to see myself writing Christian books, teaching Bible studies, participating in discipleship and ministry, leading outreach missions, or even pursuing my doctorate in biblical studies. However, I remembered what it says in Luke 1:37: *"For with God nothing will be impossible."*

The way I envisioned serving God as a young girl was not even close to what I do now. But I always had this wishful yearning to get closer to God. Perhaps my idea of serving the Lord back then was just to become a nun. It was regrettable that nobody told me about this personal relationship with God or about the Christian faith. I have a vivid recollection as a child, seeing my grandfather constantly reading his Bible. But to my astonishment, he never attended any church. Since I grew up with my grandfather, I don't recall ever having gone to church with him. I asked him about it once, and his response was about "hypocrisy at church." Those were very strange words for me. I never understood what he meant until I began to read my Bible. Sometimes, I would like to think that my grandfather must have prayed for me to carry on his unfulfilled mission to serve God. Very much attached to my grandfather—I always had inquisitive and creative thoughts that often amazed him. I was enthralled by his great stories that seemed to have lingered with my innocent, childlike curiosity. All his stories appeared to have been from the Bible.

During my late teens, I was employed by World Vision Philippines. I have a brief recollection of being introduced to the Christian faith at that time. But back then, I seemed to adhere to my old beliefs that only when you become a nun can you truly serve God. I was caught up with the daily demand of life in the fast lane. Soon, I had forgotten my yearning to serve God, except for my obligations of attending Sunday masses. I had to efface my desire to become a nun and my wishful yearning to serve the Lord when I got married. Besides, I had to immigrate to America to start a family shortly after marriage. Redirecting my full attention to raising my children and being a good housewife became my priority. Meanwhile, still not a single person reached out to my family about accepting Jesus as our Lord and Savior. Going to church every Sunday might just have been the closest I came to having access to God in my life.

It took another two decades before I would recapture that yearning to serve God. But before it could happen, though, I had to go through trials and tribulations. I became distant and detached from God. It was not an easy road to take, passing through a rocky and rugged mountain. It somehow delayed the process, but God surely paved my way to a very purposeful and godly mission in life. God became my partner in this journey of finding my life purpose. I also had to go through a series of awakening calls.

I was very much inclined to succeed in life in America, and it became my priority to do everything I could to secure our family's financial future. Bombarded by the demands of everyday living to have nice things, I began to covet those things that people usually want—a big house, a fancy car, etc. I was one of those believing in the so-called American dream—a dream that has failed many Americans. But God came to my rescue. I expressed this in a poetic prayer from my book *God Shines*.

> *God Is My Savior*
> *From the surface of my skin*
> *To the depth of my body and soul,*

*Murmuring thoughts I whisper to God,*
*I am so grateful that You rescued me from my fallen*
*world,*
*A world where I have lived long enough to become*
*subdued*
*By the things I thought were gratifying and good.*
*Consumed by my desires to have the nicest things to*
*feel alive,*
*Only to realize that these were not what I needed*
*to survive.*
*Allowing myself to be defined by the people around*
*me,*
*Wanting to prove my abilities—ones that would*
*elevate me,*
*Pride and arrogance were consuming all the energy*
*in me.*
*Thank You, God, for You came into my life to rescue*
*me. Amen.*[8]

Matthew 6:24 says, *"No one can serve two masters; for either he will hate the one and love the other, or else he will be loyal to the one and despise the other. You cannot serve God and mammon."* I didn't understand what this passage meant for quite some time, especially when I did not have a relationship with God. But this was how this passage ministered to me: we cannot claim the Lord if our allegiance is to something or someone other than Him. It was hard for me to comprehend, but it intensified by my prayer. I slowly began to instill into my heart its true meaning.

Does it mean that I have found God's true purpose for my life? I don't know. But I continually pray to God for wisdom and discernment as I stay focused on Him and His will. God is the center of my life, and my faith is rooted to <u>God's uncondit</u>ional love. My passion for living is to serve

8. Tess Paje, *God Shines* (Collierville, TN: Innovo Publishing, 2010).

God, emanated by His command and my obedience and faithfulness to Him. *"But now, O LORD, You are our Father; We are the clay, and You our potter; And all we are the work of Your hand"* (Is 64:8).

According to Oswald Chambers,

> We tend to think that if Jesus Christ compels us to do something and we are obedient to Him, He will lead us to great success. We should never have the thought that our dreams of success are God's purpose for us. In fact, His purpose may be exactly the opposite. We have the idea that God is leading us toward a particular end or a desired goal, but He is not. The question of whether or not we arrive at a particular goal is of little importance, and reaching it becomes merely an episode along the way. What we see as only the process of reaching a particular end, God sees as the goal itself.
>
> What is my vision of God's purpose for me? Whatever it may be, His purpose is for me to depend on Him and in His power now. If I can stay calm, faithful, and unconfused while in the middle of the turmoil of life, the goal of the purpose of God is being accomplished in me. God is not working toward a particular finish— His purpose is the process itself. What He desires for me is that I see "Him walking on the sea" with no shore, no success, nor goal in sight, but simply having the absolute certainty that everything is all right because I see "Him walking on the sea" (Mark 6:49). It is the process, not the outcome, that is glorifying to God.[9]

---

9. Oswald Chambers, Daily Devotional, *My Utmost for His Highest,* "God's Purpose or Mine?" https://utmost.org/god%E2%80%99s-purpose-or-mine/.

God's training is for now not later. His purpose is for this very minute, not for some time in the future. We have nothing to do with what will follow our obedience, and we are wrong to concern ourselves with it. What people call *preparation*, God sees as the goal itself. God's purpose is to enable me to see that He can walk on the storm of my life right now. If we have a further goal in mind, we are not paying enough attention to the present time. However, if we realize that moment-by-moment obedience is the goal, then each moment as it comes is precious.

We are called to serve because God wants us to take part in His work in the world.

## The Storms of Life

Being overwhelmed by great problems could cause us to meander, feeling bewildered and dejected. Disheartened by the magnitude of the problems we begin to lose control of everything around us. Hope departs as fear begins to permeate, becoming a menace to our faith. This is a typical progression when we don't allow God to control our lives. Nobody, not even Christians, is immune to the storms of life. In the book *Footsteps of Fisherman*, Scott Walker says, "Christians are not protected from the storms of life. But we can be assured that with God's help, they will not destroy us."[10] Our faith in God always brings reassurance to our safety from destruction. Proverbs 29:25 says, *"The fear of man brings a snare, but whoever trusts in the Lord shall be safe."*

A story from the book of Mark demonstrates Jesus' power to calm the raging storms. The Apostle Mark wants us to understand that when Jesus is in control, even in the midst of a great storm He will be with us to protect us. In this story, Jesus' command makes the sea keep still. Thus it encourages

---

10. Scott Walker, *Footsteps of Fisherman* (Minneapolis, MN: Augsburg Books, 2003).

us to have hope instead of fear. Jesus taught His disciples to gain insight by their experience of the actual storm. This is not something that can just be said in words. Therefore, by the power of the Holy Spirit intertwined with our faith in God, I pray this story will instill in our hearts what Jesus can and will do for us, just like what He demonstrated to His disciples.

> *On the same day, when evening had come, He said to them, "Let us cross over to the other side." Now when they had left the multitude, they took Him along in the boat as He was. And other little boats were also with Him. And a great windstorm arose, and the waves beat into the boat, so that it was already filling. But He was in the stern, asleep on a pillow. And they awoke Him and said to Him, "Teacher, do You not care that we are perishing?" Then He arose and rebuked the wind, and said to the sea, "Peace, be still!" And the wind ceased and there was a great calm. But He said to them, "Why are you so fearful? How is it that you have no faith?" And they feared exceedingly, and said to one another, "Who can this be, that even the wind and the sea obey Him!"* (Mk 4:35-41)

In his book, Scott Walker also says, "For all disciples of Jesus, it is the storms of life that provide our learning experiences. We simply cannot learn without pain and anxiety. Almost every spiritual truth that I cling to has come out of the cauldron and kiln of my own difficult moments." Indeed this is true. The storms in my life have taught me great lessons. Storms are never ending, so we should continually cling to God's promises and be totally dependent on Him. He must be the center of our lives in bad times and in good times. His promise in 2 Thessalonians 3:3 affirms it: *"But the Lord is faithful, who will establish you and guard you from the evil one."* God will give us strength and protection from Satan.

The turmoil, pain, suffering, anger, and frustration I have experienced in life prompted me to write my first book to encourage women to have hope in God. Soon after, God opened many more doors for me to serve Him. Finishing my doctorate in biblical studies was an affirmation that God had much more in store for me. During my doctoral study, my intent was to know more about Jesus, but each day that I was committed to learning about Him, the more I longed for His presence and His purpose for me. Putting closure to my past struggles was indeed a long process. But God's healing grace was my blessed assurance to heal all my brokenness. God healed my aching soul and my tainted heart. His grace was sufficient to lift my heavy baggage so I could pass through the raging waters of this fallen world. In 2 Corinthians 12:9 it says, *"My grace is sufficient for you, for My strength is made perfect in weakness."* I know that God's reassuring love and mercy will surely carry me through any challenges that come my way, whether it's relational, financial, or physical.

> *When troubles come our way*
> *Call on God for grace and mercy*
> *To redeem us and restore us*
> *To love us and sustain us*
> *When our fear comes like a storm*
> *When our pain comes like a whirlwind*
> *When anxiety and anguish come upon us*
> *Call on God for wisdom to strengthen us*

Overcoming the storms of life can be difficult, and the process may be long. Pains and suffering can impair your strength physically, emotionally, and spiritually. If you face uncertainty about your future, lean on God, the One who foresees the future in detail. Leaving your comfort zone to live in the faith zone can create for you a greater purpose. It can lead you to a daily encounter with the living God.

Moses was the greatest role model of faith. According to the book *Running with the Giants,* Moses overcame his experiences (past, present, future) by stepping out of his comfort zone to live a life of faith. First, "Moses overcame the experience of his past." Having been born into uncertainty, he was taken in by Pharaoh's daughter to live a life of comfort. But then, he had to flee everything he'd ever known after killing an Egyptian to defend a fellow Hebrew. Second, "Moses overcame the comfort of his present." After Moses left Egypt, he spent time in the wilderness of Midian tending sheep. He grew accustomed to the lifestyle there. The desert became another safe zone for Moses. Jethro took him in and made him part of his family. Moses took one of Jethro's daughters as his wife and they had a son. Third, "Moses overcame the insecurity of his future." Moses was insecure about himself and his future when God called him to leave his comfortable situation and go back to Egypt to deliver children of Israel out of the hands of Pharaoh.[11]

These lessons from the life of Moses are great examples of what God can and will do for us if we are obedient and surrender to His will and purpose for our lives. Moses' godly encounter from his birth where his life was spared, his burning-bush encounter with God, the parting of the Red Sea, receiving the Ten Commandments, and leading the children of Israel out of Egypt demonstrates the power of our living God. We must learn from Moses' life of faith to help us conquer our own storms of life. When you think you're not the right person to do God's mission, pray for wisdom, as we are called to, and be prepared to step out of your comfort zone and start to live in the faith zone.

---

11. John C. Maxwell, *Running with the Giants* (Nashville: Faith-Words, 2003), 41–43.

M—*Most loving Father, we offer*
O—*Our life to You in full trust*
S—*Stepping out of our comfort zone*
E—*Entrusting You by faith*
S—*Storms of life You shall defeat. Amen.*

As we live our Christian lives to the fullest, we must continue moving forward. Let's look at more opportunities to help us do this.

# Are We Moving On as Christians?

The purpose of this chapter is to help us grow and move on as Christians. We must stay focused on our loving Father and continue to run the race of faith. This is Step Five in our journey with God. This part of the journey opens up opportunities to explore while we run the race of faith. And it may very well happen that you unleash your potential to lead; after all, we believers are called to lead. Let us pray that God will continue to sustain us and lift our worries, concerns, and challenges to His mighty power.

## Running the Race of Faith

In 2 Timothy 4:7 it says, *"I have fought the good fight, I have finished the race, I have kept the faith."* The Apostle Paul is referring to the end of his ministry. He remained faithful and obedient to the Lord. So must we. Running the race of faith is an image for living the Christian life. It portrays how well we obey God's truth and our faithfulness to Him. True Christians always strive to run the race of faith and finish it well. Sometimes, we can become distracted with so many things in this world that it causes us to stumble and fall. Be reminded that Galatians 5:7 says, *"You were running a good race. Who cut in on you to keep you from obeying the truth?"* Are you running a good race? If not, then why?

I remember when I was new in my faith. I was with a group of new believers who were all fired up in their walk with the Lord. I thought we were all headed for a good start to run the race of faith. Unfortunately, a few years down the road, some did not grow in their relationship with Jesus. Some of them went back to their old selves or just became complacent with their lifestyles.

What happened here reminded me of Jesus' parable of the soil/sower in Matthew 13:3-9:

> *Then He spoke many things to them in parables, saying: "Behold, a sower went out to sow. And as he sowed, some seed fell by the wayside; and the birds came and devoured them. Some fell on stony places, where they did not have much earth; and they immediately sprang up because they had no depth of earth. But when the sun was up they were scorched, and because they had no root they withered away. And some fell among thorns, and the thorns sprang up and choked them. But others fell on good ground and yielded a crop: some a hundredfold, some sixty, some thirty. He who has ears to hear, let him hear!"*

This is the explanation of this parable taken from the New Living Translation:

> *Now listen to the explanation of the parable about the farmer planting seeds: The seed that fell on*

*the footpath represents those who hear the message about the Kingdom and don't understand it. Then the evil one comes and snatches away the seed that was planted in their hearts. The seed on the rocky soil represents those who hear the message and immediately receive it with joy. But since they don't have deep roots, they don't last long. They fall away as soon as they have problems or are persecuted for believing God's word. The seed that fell among the thorns represents those who hear God's word, but all too quickly the message is crowded out by the worries of this life and the lure of wealth, so no fruit is produced. The seed that fell on good soil represents those who truly hear and understand God's word and produce a harvest of thirty, sixty, or even a hundred times as much as had been planted!* (Mt 13:18-23 NLT).

It should be your heart's desire to be the seed that fell on good soil. After accepting Jesus as your Lord and Savior, you should want to grow and be spiritually matured in your personal relationship with God. We then have a desire to hear, understand, and apply His Word for His kingdom to come to our hearts and for His will to be done in us. I was so burdened by the fact that as I continued running the race of faith, I was leaving behind some of my family and friends. However, I always pray for them that someday they may enter the race. It took my husband a long time before he would run the race of faith again.

Our goal is to win the prize. It is what motivates us. Running the race with no goal will not allow Jesus to come into our lives. It will not get us anywhere, and this is not what Jesus wants. We need to be prepared. We need to equip ourselves with the truth. The gospel is the truth. Ephesians 6:13-20 says,

> *Therefore take up the whole armor of God, that you may be able to withstand in the evil day, and having done all, to stand. Stand therefore, having girded your waist with truth, having put on the breastplate of righteousness, and having shod your feet with the preparation of the gospel of peace; above all, taking the shield of faith with which you will be able to quench all the fiery darts of the wicked one. And take the helmet of salvation, and the sword of the Spirit, which is the word of God; praying always with all prayer and supplication in the Spirit, being watchful to this end with all perseverance and supplication for all the saints—and for me, that utterance may be given to me, that I may open my mouth boldly to make known the mystery of the gospel, for which I am an ambassador in chains; that in it I may speak boldly, as I ought to speak.*

The Apostle Paul emphasized the necessity of spiritual armor: girdle or belt of truth, breastplate of righteousness, shoes to prepare you for the gospel of peace. Being truthful, righteous, and ready to spread the good news is the basic uniform we need to wear at all times. However, when we are in the battlefield, we must also protect ourselves by using the shield of faith, helmet of salvation, and sword of the Spirit. The shield of faith refers to our full and continual trust in God to protect us from all kinds of sins. The helmet of salvation or helmet of the hope of salvation refers to our assurance of eternal life, and we need to be strong in the promises of God. The sword of the Spirit refers to God's Word, which is the truth. Ephesians 6:19 also emphasizes the power of prayer, such that we need to pray always as we submit to the will of God.

Until the Lord returns, we must stand firm against the enemy without falling into his trap. To continue running the race of faith, we pray for boldness and faithfulness as we proclaim the gospel to the unsaved no matter what it costs.

We must stay on course by constantly reading the Word of God and staying in daily prayer. Hebrews 12:1 says, *"Therefore, since we are surrounded by such a great cloud of witnesses, let us throw off everything that hinders and the sin that so easily entangles. And let us run with perseverance the race marked out for us."* The discipline of faith helps us to persevere, but we must push away evil thoughts and practices, for they will greatly hinder us from finishing the race.

According to Pastor John McArthur,

> The entrance to the race is the new birth, salvation by faith in the perfect and complete work of Christ. And apart from faith in Christ, you're not even in the race. You're on the sideline. The race starts for you when you become a believer. But once you become a believer, you must be continually urged and Paul does that, as we pointed out, a number of times to run with all your might . . . not to jog, not to walk, not to sit down and rest, not to fall back. The Holy Spirit is calling us to run.[12]

Running the race of faith is a long process, and getting started requires us to be rightly related to Jesus, which is the beginning of a lifetime commitment to God. To be rightly related to Jesus, first and foremost, we must receive Jesus as our Lord and Savior and then continue to grow and mature in our walk with Him. With the power of the Holy Spirit, as we seek and trust God, He will sustain us, allowing us to continue running the race of faith.

In running the race of faith, we also need to remember to encourage those around us in their race. Philippians 2:2

---

12. Pastor John McArthur, "The Race of Faith," http://www.gty. org/resources/sermons/90-390/the-race-of-faith.

says, *"Fulfill my joy by being like-minded, having the same love, being of one accord, of one mind."* Henceforth, we are one body in Christ, and together we come in one accord to fulfill God's purpose for our lives. True believers are called to lead people to God, and our determination to run the race of faith could encourage others to do the same. In 1 Thessalonians 5:11 it says, *"Therefore encourage one another and build each other up, just as in fact you are doing."* When we run together, we feel more secured that someone is there to help us when we fall. God created us to fellowship with one another, and together we'll embark on a greater purpose with godly insight for direction and guidance.

Being one body in Christ, each part of the body has to function in order to accomplish what it was made for. *"Who comforts us in all our troubles, so that we can comfort those in any trouble with the comfort we ourselves receive from God"* (2 Cor 1:4).

In retrospect, our commonality, oneness, and solidity to one another will make our dreams a reality; our unity for God's purpose will bring honor and glory to our heavenly Father. Together we must pursue the Great Commission as spoken about in Matthew 28:19-20: *"Therefore go and make disciples of all nations, baptizing them in the name of the Father and of the Son and of the Holy Spirit, and teaching them to obey everything I have commanded you. And surely I am with you always, to the very end of the age."*

During the race, we will be consistently tested for the validity of our faith. There will be challenges as well as rewards. But the ultimate reward is unsurpassable; it is eternity in heaven. As noted by the title of this book, *A Journey to a Spirit-Filled Life*, we each have responsibilities and accountabilities. Philippians 3:14 (NIV) says, *"I press on toward the goal to win the prize for which God has called me heavenward in Christ Jesus."*

Pastor McArthur says, "You know, you're in a race; keep your eyes off the ground, off your feet, off your surroundings. Where do we put our eyes? We put our eyes on Christ." Indeed, we all know that Jesus is the author and finisher of our faith; thus He is the ultimate model of faith. Jesus is the same yesterday, today, and forever. Therefore, we must fix our eyes on Jesus as we emulate His life, teachings, and example in order to finish the race and finish it well. Are you running with purpose? If so, then you are taking your life into a new level of faith, unleashing your potential to lead.

## Unleashing Our Potential to Lead

Unleashing our potential to lead is about being able to accept the challenge of living fully and realizing our dreams to lead people to God as we seek divine guidance through prayer and His Word. All Christians are called to lead. The true calling of a Christian is to lead out of obedience to God's call.

In unleashing our potential to lead, we become aware of the uniqueness of our thinking, feeling, speaking, and doing. As we become aware of these unique personal powers, we need to claim them as being from God and put them to use to become godly leaders. God is honored and exalted when we use our personal powers to glorify Him.

Christian leadership can happen anywhere at any time, whether it's in the home, the workplace, or the community. The real test of true leadership is applying the concept of leadership in your own life first and then in the lives of others. Here are some of the concepts to consider: Are you personally and passionately committed to leadership? How important is it for you to lead? Does it require a transformation in you and your lifestyle? Does it have to happen now, or can you afford to wait? Have you sought the leading of God?

God's command, His way, His vision, and His great love for us are perfect, absolute, permanent, and limitless; therefore, true leadership begins with God. The Scripture in Deuteronomy 32:4 says, *"He is the Rock, His work is perfect; For all His ways are justice."* Indeed, God's Word is a great source of guiding practices and principles and is always made available to us. Having a personal goal and spiritual wisdom with genuine vision complemented with God-given enthusiasm and unyielding confidence will enable us to unleash our potential to lead. There's always a need for Christian leaders who are able to help clearly explain the essential truths of Christianity—Christian leaders who can provide biblical counsel with deep human and spiritual insight.

True leadership requires full submission, surrender, and obedience to His deity; this should be where every believer begins his good work. By emulating Jesus' teachings and examples, we will be guided by the truth—truth that gives us freedom. Jesus said in John 15:15, *"No longer do I call you servants, for a servant does not know what his master is doing; but I have called you friends, for all things that I heard from My Father I have made known to you."*

## Attributes of a Christian Leader

It is important to get familiar with the following attributes of a Christian leader as we seek to unleash our potential to lead. They will be our guiding principles and practices that can help us structure our leadership style.

### 1. OUR ACCOUNTABILITY

As Christian leaders, we must apply accountability in all areas of our lives. We need to be honest and trustworthy, making sure that we behave the same in public as we would when no one sees us. It was said in Romans 14:12, *"So then each of us shall give account of himself to God."* It clearly states that we are preordained to God's ultimate judgment. Therefore, we will only give full account of ourselves to our heavenly Father. We are able to give a full account for ourselves because we have sole control of our own actions. There may be things that are not seen by others, but God will see everything. Ultimately, God will hold us accountable for our actions. Therefore, we should have standards and structure that provide boundaries for accountability because it is easy to be deceived, and how we appear to others can have great influence on others and how we lead.

Accountability to God is one of the most important attributes of a Christian leader. Christian leaders should be accountable for their dependability, decisiveness, endurance, tact, loyalty, integrity, faithfulness to God, and obedience to God's command. As Christian leaders, our lives are meant to model and teach; otherwise, we fail. In 2 Corinthians 13:5 it says, *"Examine yourselves to see if your faith is genuine. Test yourselves. Surely you know that Jesus Christ is among you; if not, you have failed the test of genuine faith."* Having said that, who are you truly accountable to?

We are solely liable, responsible, and answerable to God for our own actions. In 2 Corinthians 5:10 (NKJV) it says, *"For we must all appear before the judgment seat of Christ, that each one may receive the things done in the body, according to what he has done, whether good or bad."* Similarly, we are also accountable to our fellow Christians to hold to their belief so they are not distracted, discouraged, or confused on their path. *"Let each of you look out not only for his own interests, but also for the interests of others"* (Phil 2:4 NKJV).

Oftentimes, Christian leaders overlook accountability in some areas of their lives. Even though they have a lot of exposure regarding their accountability, especially around temptations, they have access—in the Word of God—to resist temptation, just as Jesus did. Christian leadership depends highly on examining Jesus' leadership. We are expected to conduct ourselves with absolute honesty, integrity, humility, and commitment in the way we act and perform our responsibilities. Accountability should be our true essence of living, guided by God's faithfulness, truthfulness, and righteousness as emanated by the Holy Spirit. In spite of challenges, turmoil, or disease, we conquer, as Romans 8:35, 37 (NLT) says, *"Can anything ever separate us from Christ's love? Does it mean he no longer loves us if we have trouble or calamity, or are persecuted, or hungry, or destitute, or in danger, or threatened with death? No, despite all these things, overwhelming victory is ours through Christ, who loved us."*

## 2. OUR BELIEF IN GOD AND DEPENDENCE ON GOD

The very core of our biblical principle is our belief in God as we seek to discover His Word, understand the truths, and apply the message. The psalmist in Psalm 119:105 said, *"Your word is a lamp to my feet and a light to my path."* We know that God spoke His message through the people who authored the Bible in order to show us the highest moral standard in history—the life of Jesus Christ. Indeed, Jesus' sacrificial death portrayed God's plan to humanity, which is to rescue us from the bondage of our sinful nature. It is important to read the Bible with prayerful dependency on the Holy Spirit to speak to our hearts as we are willing to submit to God's moral direction. God, through the Bible, will communicate with us, and when we read and apply God's Word regularly, we will start to see the world in a Christian way. It brings living messages to us with the power to transform our lives and character that can change our whole perspective on dealing with life as a whole and will carry us to a higher level of Christian leadership.

When we believe and trust God, we become dependent on Him. Our goal then is to be dependent upon God's resources rather than our own. The Bible says do not be afraid, do not worry about your life, or do not be anxious for anything, but let your request be made known to God, and the peace of God will guard your hearts and minds. The peace of God given to us carries with it a sense of peace that can withstand tremendous challenges. With Jesus' life modeling His dependence on the Father, this can also teach us how to go about embracing that mindset of peace and tranquility. Worrying will not change the reality of life, and by worrying, it's just going to distract us.

Therefore, take refuge in God, and seek His presence in everything you do. Our trust and hopes should be vested in God. Allow Him to be in control of unleashing your potential to lead.

## 3. OUR CHARACTER

The character of a Christian leader speaks a lot about his leadership abilities. Humility, integrity, compassion, trustworthiness, honesty, faithfulness, obedience, forgiveness, and truthfulness are genuine qualities built from within a leader. These are leadership skills that shape a Christian leader to conform to God's purpose and His call to leadership.

Humility is the willingness to submit to the greater wisdom of the One from whom all things come. The focus of humility is not on oneself but on God. In Philippians 2:3-4, Paul wrote, *"Do nothing out of selfish ambition or vain conceit, but in humility consider others better than yourselves. Each of you should look not only to your own interests, but also to the interests of others."* Jesus' death on the cross for our sins is the best representation of humility. As Christian leaders, we need to emulate Jesus' humility. If we are truly humble, we must remove the things that promote pride as pointed out in Proverbs 11:2: *"When pride comes, then comes disgrace, but with humility comes wisdom."* Pride is a barrier between God and man.

A high degree of integrity is demanded in a Christian leader. There must be a consistency between what is inside us and what is outside us. How we live and act determine our true character and the reflection of God in our lives. Character development in the area of integrity carries a great deal of trust and moral/ethical values.

## 4. OUR COMMITMENT AND PASSION

Commitment intertwined with passion will help us unleash our potential to lead. It is our passion that makes us committed to do the things we want to do and the things that we value the most. Our commitment to lead is to the living God. Our true success flows out of a radical commitment to Him. Proverbs 16:3 says, *"Commit your works to the Lord and your thoughts will be established."* With our total trust and submission to the will of God, He will fulfill our righteous plans. We want our lives to have passion for the things that God has declared are important because of His commitment to us. Christian leaders are empowered with confidence, courage, and endurance, all because of the power of the Holy Spirit that abides in us.

# Leadership Styles

The aforementioned attributes must intertwine with the following leadership styles. These are distinct, embedded qualities of Christian leaders that separate them from those being led: God-given mission and vision, that which recognizes a divine intervention; godly driven values, that which deals with personal conviction; and purposeful priorities, that which infuses God's purpose and will for them.

## 1. GOD-GIVEN MISSION AND VISION

2 Corinthians 4:16-18 says,

> *Therefore we do not lose heart. Even though our outward man is perishing, yet the inward man is being renewed day by day. For our light affliction, which is but for a moment, is working for us a far more exceeding and eternal weight of glory, while we do not look at the things which are seen, but at the things which are not seen. For the things which are seen are temporary, but the things which are not seen are eternal.*

Christian leaders need to understand that in the midst of all adversities and worries that seem to engulf our whole being and tend to wear us out, we should not lose heart. Through God's love and mercy, we will continue to grow and mature with Him. God's promises will sustain us and strengthen us throughout the mission as our vision continues to prosper us.

Letting God authenticate our quest to unleash our potential to lead will affirm our relationship with Him. Remember, Jesus preordained all Christians to pursue the Great Commission as told in Matthew 28:19-20: *"Go therefore and make disciples of all the nations, baptizing them in the name of the Father and of the Son and of the Holy Spirit, teaching them to observe all things that I have commanded you; and lo, I am with you always, even to the end of the age. Amen."* Empowered by God's principles and practices, it will carry us to a deliberate and purposeful missionary "take-off" in order to fulfill this Great Commission.

When we clearly understand that we are all aliens on the earth and we see that the rewards are not on the earth, then our focus and our hope will be in God. Therefore, we should ask God to give us vision to illuminate our paths.

Remember, we are still walking in faith until we walk in light when we see God face to face.

## 2. GODLY DRIVEN VALUES

Our clear set of godly driven values will help us navigate the Christian leadership process in order to not lose contact with those we are leading. It promotes commonality, unity, and solidity in our organization to work together, making it less likely for anyone to wander.

Truthfulness, kindness, integrity, honesty, and justice are values that help motivate us to a higher calling and conviction. In our hearts, these values speak truth. Values that are God-driven will shape up our personal conviction where no matter what happens, there's a feeling of stability in our personal, relational, and spiritual pursuits.

Emulate Jesus' love and treasure what He declares is important. Doing things that are pleasing to Him and honoring Him with your life will give you your true identity and reveal your leadership calling. Seek God in your heart, and trust that you will get the core power of leadership that is imbedded in God's Word. Matthew 6:21 says, *"For where your treasure is, there your heart will be also."* There is a potential danger of our possessions becoming our idols. We should not let our material possessions become a spiritual hindrance in leading God's people. Our godly driven values will determine our priorities.

## 3. PURPOSEFUL PRIORITIES

God has called every believer to a specific area that He purposely designed for them. It was said in Exodus 31:3, *"And I have filled him with the Spirit of God, in wisdom, in understanding, in knowledge, and in all manner of workmanship."* God filled us with wisdom, understanding, knowledge, and workmanship uniquely designed to find our own identity in Him. We each have a special place in God. Jeremiah 29:11 says, *"For I know the thoughts that I think toward you,' says the Lord, 'thoughts of peace and not evil, to give you a hope and a future. Then you will call upon Me and go and pray to Me, and I will listen to you. And you will seek Me and find Me, when you search for Me with all your heart.'"* This is our call for a divine appointment with God. Are you ready to make that appointment a priority?

Romans 11:36 says, *"For of Him and through Him and to Him are all things, to whom be glory forever. Amen."* We therefore acknowledge that God is the source of everything. We also believe that He sustains things for us. Ultimately, we understand that the rightful end of all things belongs to Him. Are we then living for Him, with Him, and through Him? Are the priorities we set in life aligned with that of God's purpose?

We have purpose just as God does, but our purpose here on earth is limited and temporary. God's purpose for us includes everything that is permanent. In God's providence, He orchestrates everything associated with our lives in order for Him to work within us and bring the best in us as we become faithful and obedient to His will and purpose. Romans 8:28 affirms this truth: *"And we know that all things work together for good to those who love God, to those who are the called according to His purpose."* God called each Christian to lead, and His calling is in accordance with His will. So, are we responding to this call out of obedience to God?

Somehow, man has the tendency to become dwellers of the temporal, to the things that come with easy access, which are gratifying to man's lust of material or physical possessions. This happens to many leaders who are in the position of being over others who have a self-seeking interest and selfish personal desires. It's very unfortunate for them to fall into this trap because it means their priorities are not set for godly living. The Law of God is a valuable source revealing divine guidance and provision to help Christian leaders from faltering.

# Leadership Challenge

Unleashing our potential to lead is not an easy task. Crises will challenge our leadership capacity and can damage us personally or damage our organization, our community, and especially our relationship with God. Challenges are inevitable, but temporary. *"For as the heavens are higher than the earth, So are My ways higher than your ways, And My thoughts than your thoughts"* (Is 55:9). This verse speaks of God's supremacy over man as the ruler of everything. Therefore, only with God can we be secured in our leadership challenges.

We need to face some common and repeatedly abused leadership challenges. I would like to reinforce some foundational biblical principles and practices relating to each of these challenges. This is an opportunity for leaders to recall what it means to lead like Jesus, with the understanding and application of Jesus' servant-focused leadership.

John 13:13-17 says,

> *You call Me Teacher and Lord, and you say well, for so I am. If I then, your Lord and Teacher, have washed your feet, you also ought to wash one another's feet. For I have given you an example, that you should do as I have done to you. Most assuredly, I say to you, a servant is not greater than his master; nor is he who is sent greater than he who sent him. If you know these things, blessed are you if you do them.*

Jesus' purpose in washing the feet of His disciples was to establish the model of loving humility and therefore set an example for them about the true meaning of servant leadership. When Jesus died on the cross and cried out to the Father in Luke 23:46, *"Father, into Your hands I commit My spirit,"* He simply yielded His soul—a reflection of His obedience to the Father. He was committed to a perfect relationship with the Father, which means that a relationship with God is one of the greatest challenges in Christian leadership.

Establishing a relationship with Jesus carries a high degree of obedience and faithfulness to His deity, power, and dominion, as it is the core foundation of Christian leadership. Some Christian leaders fail to obey God and remain focused on their self-seeking interests and personal desires. Obedience to God and His commands enhanced by frequent reading and meditating of His Word coupled with prayer and application of His teachings will deter wicked thoughts and deeds, thus restoring and developing leadership in you.

Another leadership challenge relates to Christian leaders wanting to compromise with the things that are not spiritual in nature. Unfortunately, many Christian leaders don't practice what they preach. *"Therefore put to death your members which are on the earth: fornication, uncleanness, passion, evil desire, and covetousness, which is idolatry"* (Col 3:5). Idolatry is putting our longings in place of God; this is blasphemy. The lure of material possessions and uncontrolled, lavish lifestyles can be a form of idolatry. As an antidote to idolatry, we must put God at the center of our daily living.

In general, people like to compromise in matters that satisfy the longing of the flesh—things of the world. It is alarming that the material world can be such a powerful force to program people's minds into being attracted to everything worldly, drawing their hearts into the ungodly desires of power, wealth, and fame and therefore drawing them farther away from the things of God. This is not to say that a godly person cannot have wealth or material possessions; they indeed can. It becomes ungodly when the focus is on "stuff" rather than God. Money is not evil; but the love—or lust—of money is evil. Until we fully submit our allegiance to God's sovereign power, these things will direct our focus away from unleashing our potential to lead.

In John 14:6, Jesus said, *"I am the way, the truth, and the life. No one comes to the Father except through Me."* This indicates that Jesus is the *only* way to the Father because He is the truth and life of God. Therefore, we must place our absolute trust in Him to supply our needs and not the temporary things of this world. In his book *Ruthless Trust*, Brennan Manning said, "Ruthless trust is an unerring sense, way deep down that beneath the surface agitation, boredom, and insecurities of life, it's gonna be all right. The wind may blow, more character defect may surface, sickness may visit, and friends will surely die, but the stubborn, irrefutable certainty persists that God is with us and loves us in our struggle to be faithful."[13]

Author Michael Card speaks about Peter who became a devoted friend and completely dependent on Jesus, even though he eventually stumbled, lost his temper, said no to Jesus, and denied Him. "There comes a point in our lives when all the pieces of our past, both good and bad, come together to make a meaningful whole."[14] Indeed, it made a lot of sense to Peter to walk away from being a fisherman to becoming a fisher of men.

As Christian leaders, we too can be fishers of men like Peter. Is this something that you envisioned for your life? Please pray about it and ask God for discernment. I hope that each day, as we walk by faith in our relationship with Jesus, we continue to move on as Christians. Then, as we run the race of faith, we are determined to finish it well. Henceforth, the goal in our journey is centered on God's glory.

---

13. Brennan Manning, *Ruthless Trust* (New York: HarperCollins, 2009).
14. Michael Card, *A Fragile Stone* (Westmont, IL: InterVarsity Press, 2006).

# STEP SIX

# Are We Bound for Heaven?

I n asking the question, *Are we bound for heaven?*—we can determine how well we are doing as Christians and how we should live now in readiness for the next life. We need to have a constant goal in life; otherwise, we are prone to drift and are never satisfied. For us Christians, our ultimate goal in life is to glorify God and to spend eternity in heaven. Therefore, every thought, word, and deed should be the true representation of God and His kingdom. We must prepare ourselves, for we do not know when the Son of man will arrive.

This is Step Six, the final step in our journey with God. In this concluding journey, we will explore the following: (1) How to stay on course on the road to heaven and not wander or get sidetracked; (2) How to stay focused in our lifetime commitment to serve God and others; and (3) How do we hope to live and conclude our life here on earth? Are we hopeful that our mission here on earth will be accomplished, or shall we remain a work in progress until we come to our permanent home?

# On the Road to Heaven

It is a long and winding road to heaven and indeed a lifelong process. Philippians 3:20 says, *"For our citizenship is in heaven, from which we also eagerly wait for the Savior, the Lord Jesus Christ."* Since our citizenship is in heaven, we need to stay on course on the road to heaven. We are all imperfect people. But we can lean on those with greater spiritual maturity to help us in the process of pursuing a godly life. As leaders, we also need to be that source of spiritual maturity for others.

The Apostle Paul was such a model. He warned believers not to set their minds on earthly things because they belong to our heavenly Father. Heaven is the home of believers; it is where God dwells and where Jesus Christ is present. John 14:2-3 says, *"In My Father's house are many mansions; if it were not so, I would have told you. I go to prepare a place for you. And if I go and prepare a place for you, I will come again and receive you to Myself; that where I am, there you may be also."* Believers will be taken from earth to live in heaven where their names are registered and their inheritance awaits. Be reminded to meditate upon these two verses, and ask God to let the hope of heaven encourage us as we walk in confidence with Him.

Believers always view heaven as their permanent home. Once you recognize that Jesus' death on the cross was God's way of offering forgiveness and paving the way for your eternal life, then you will become confident that you are bound for heaven. By the power of the Holy Spirit, we can change our sinful nature into something pure, honest, and humble. Hopefully, we will recognize how important our lives are here on earth because it is here where we come to terms with God's plan and purpose for each of us. The Bible is our road map to heaven.

Unfortunately, many of us live as if this present life on earth is all that matters. We focus our time and energy on acquiring what this fallen world has to offer. We have a tendency to become dwellers of the temporal instead of the eternal. Such an attitude about life becomes an attitude about death. When death approaches, there may be fear as one becomes conscious of all their sins, hasty words, and unkind actions and reactions. Remember, repentance is never too late. Don't miss out on the joy of reconciliation.

I believe that as you follow Step One through Step Six in this book, it will help you grow and mature in your personal relationship with God, and it will help you gain a deeper understanding of the relevancy in your daily activities. Think about a concrete block whereby grains of sand need to be combined with the concrete mix to create a block. Each grain of sand collectively represents our day-to-day activities that are godly driven. When combined with concrete mix, which represents God's blessings, it creates a solid foundation of Christian faith. With each day, honoring and trusting God gives meaning to His purpose. We then focus on fulfilling God's promises in order to achieve His plan and purpose. This process helps us to persevere through the raging waters and bumpy road that leads to heaven.

Matthew 7:13-14 (NIV) says, *"Enter through the narrow gate. For wide is the gate and broad is the road that leads to destruction, and many enter through it. But small is the gate and narrow the road that leads to life, and only a few find it."* Jesus' sacrificial death was meant to plead to people to choose the narrow gate, which is God's gate, the only gate to heaven. However, we were given two choices on how we want to live our lives, each with different judgments. The broad gate includes all religious practices and self-righteousness, which leads to destruction, whereas the narrow gate calls for knowledge of the truth that requires repentance and submission to Jesus, which leads to eternal life. On the road to heaven, passing through the narrow gate requires self-denial; we can't carry the baggage of sin and self-will. Don't be mindful of the things of the world but only of the things that are godly.

As we make every effort to be on the road to heaven, Jesus wants us to express and enjoy our oneness here on earth. As Christians, we want the world to see our love for each other as a representation of God in order for them to be encouraged to take our message seriously. Heaven is beyond our imagination, but our faith in Jesus' promises will bring assurance that one day He is coming back to earth. Meditate upon the following Scripture about heaven:

> *Whom have I in heaven but You? And there is none upon earth that I desire besides You.* (Ps 73:25)

> *Thus says the Lord: "Heaven is My throne, And earth is My footstool. Where is the house that you will build Me? And where is the place of My rest?"* (Is 66:1)

> *In this manner, therefore, pray: "Our Father in heaven, Hallowed be Your name. Your kingdom come, Your will be done On earth as it is in heaven."* (Mt 6:9-10)

## Service for Life

Christians are called to share in the work that God has been doing on this earth. Romans 8:28 says, *"And we know that all things work together for good to those who love God, to those who are the called according to His purpose."* God orchestrates every event in your life as He calls you to fulfill

His great purpose. This call of His great purpose is to bring salvation to all sinners. Through Jesus' redemptive sufferings and death on the cross, we have been saved, and by the power of the Holy Spirit we received wisdom through faith to do whatever God wants. It is to be understood that as Christians, we ought to present Christ's person and work in evangelism—sharing the gospel with others so they too can receive salvation.

Part of being a Christian is our commitment and willingness to serve God and serve others. Indeed, Christian service is an act of faith. Therefore, we need to grow in faith as 2 Peter 1:3-4 (NLT) describes:

> *By his divine power, God has given us everything we need for living a godly life. We have received all of this by coming to know him, the one who called us to himself by means of his marvelous glory and excellence. And because of his glory and excellence, he has given us great and precious promises. These are the promises that enable you to share his divine nature and escape the world's corruption caused by human desires.*

As true believers, and being secured in our salvation, Jesus is our source of divine power to grow in faith, persevere, and become sufficient to sustain a godly life. Living a godly life also means we become good stewards of our time, talents, abilities, and resources, and use them for our Christian service.

As we render our services to others, we must not depend only on our human ideas and methods but instead allow God's Spirit to dwell in us, being controlled by His Word. God's Word is the truth of His nature that carries the authority vested in us that should never be doubted. It is the infinite wealth of wisdom from God's Word that gives

Christian service its strength, newness, and vigor. The Bible equips the Christian for battle. Having the knowledge that is in the Bible is our weapon of spiritual power that protects and sustains us. As we are called to be fruitful in service, bearing Christ's message and the compassion to act upon a needy world, we need to pray for His guidance, protection, and provision to empower us. Taking every opportunity for service is a lifetime commitment.

Compelled by the love of God, Christians are committed to letting God work in their lives in His way, which is perfect. *"As for God, His way is perfect; The word of the LORD is proven; He is a shield to all who trust in Him"* (2 Sm 22:31). Trusting God to direct us will surely help us grow more sensitive to the needs of others as we serve them. Our concern for others makes a purposeful and meaningful service; thus we need to emulate Jesus' life and examples.

Matthew 14:14 depicts Jesus' concern and service for others: *"And when Jesus went out He saw a great multitude, and He was moved with compassion for them, and healed their sick."* Because of Jesus' great love for His Father, He was faithful and obedient to do God's will; thus Jesus is our greatest role model of servanthood. Christian service must be driven by the love of God that has been poured out in our hearts through Jesus' redemptive act and by the power of God's Spirit.

The Holy Spirit plays a significant role in promoting purposeful and successful Christian service through our endless prayer. When we pray, we draw near to God. Prayer is a vital part of our relationship with God through Jesus Christ. It is a way of Christian life to be able to access our divine appointment with God and thereby allow us to carry out His will and service in this world. Prayer is one very important aspect of Christian service because it brings God into the inner core of our spiritual being. Through prayer, God can penetrate into the heart of every human emotion and experience, allowing Him to mold and develop the best in us for His glory. Prayer is also an expression of worship, thanksgiving, confession, and intercession to God.

There are many Christian-based organizations that render services, as there are plenty of personal opportunities to service other people. But be certain that these services should be centered on God because He is the only One whom we serve. We should work with enthusiasm as though we were working for the Lord rather than for people. From the smallest to the grandest services that we provide to others, represent our love, obedience, and faithfulness to God. God has provided us with unique talents, abilities, and resources to be able to carry out our services in different arenas. However, they must all be disseminated to give praise, honor, and glory to God.

Ephesians 6:5-9 speaks of a bondservant and a master's duty to each other to be obedient and respectful—this is in reference to an employee/employer relationship. There should be respect of authority with genuine sincerity as if one was serving Christ Himself. To serve one's employers well is to serve Christ well. Indeed, there should be mutual respect from employees and employers. An employer's authority and power must be given with justice and grace to honor our heavenly Master.

> *Bondservants, be obedient to those who are your masters according to the flesh, with fear and trembling, in sincerity of heart, as to Christ; not with eyeservice, as men-pleasers, but as bondservants of Christ, doing the will of God from the heart, with goodwill doing service, as to the Lord, and not to men, knowing that whatever good anyone does, he will receive the same from the Lord, whether he is a slave or free. And you, masters, do the same things to them, giving up threatening, knowing that your own*

*Master also is in heaven, and there is no partiality with Him.* (Eph 6:5-9)

In everything you do to serve God and others, always allow God to control all situations. One of the most common services we do as Christians is in the mission field in other countries. Many things can go wrong, especially when we're away from home, but leaving the leading to God will secure the mission. In doing so, we minister directly to our Lord. Our willingness to move out of our comfort zone and serve God is what ministry is all about, and through faith, it will create a realization of who we are in Christ. Indeed, through His great and mighty power, and because of our conviction, we will live out our lives in Him.

Our deeds complement our faith, as James 2:14-17 says:

> *What good is it, my brothers and sisters, if someone claims to have faith but has no deeds? Can such faith save them? Suppose a brother or a sister is without clothes and daily food. If one of you says to them, "Go in peace; keep warm and well fed," but does nothing about their physical needs, what good is it? In the same way, faith by itself, if it is not accompanied by action, is dead. The evidence of faith is through works—though all righteous behavior conforms to the Word of God—which is the act of being compassionate to others with action.*

Christian service has helped transform the world through the different outreach ministries, as we are reminded to do in the Great Commission in Matthew 28:18-20: *"Then Jesus came to them and said, 'All authority in heaven and on earth has been given to me. Therefore go and make disciples of all nations, baptizing them in the name of the Father and of the Son and of the Holy Spirit, and teaching them to obey everything*

*I have commanded you. And surely I am with you always, to the very end of the age.'"* Absolute sovereign authority in heaven and on earth was handed to Jesus; God exalted Him above all. On the basis of this authority, the disciples were sent to make disciples in all nations. Through Jesus as God's perfect servant, God fulfilled all His plans for the world. God's redemption for all our sins was done for us by the death of Jesus on the cross. This makes Jesus the greatest author and promoter of Christian service. As followers of Jesus Christ, our service is to be worked out in all areas of family life and social concern.

Service is a ministry rendered to God or to people. Serving our one true God blesses us in so many ways. While His blessings are often material, we cannot assume they will always be so, and the likelihood may not be immediate. It may be spiritual rather than physical blessings, and it may not even happen until we go to our permanent home with our heavenly Father. Our service is a lifetime commitment. We should not simply do things for ourselves but help others who can continue after us, taking God's work to its next level.

## Mission Accomplished

We all have our missions to accomplish in life. Though more often than not, we remain a work in progress. But for the most part, we Christians always aim to finish the race of life well. Jesus' mission for God was affirmed "mission accomplished" when He died. The death of Jesus in John 19:28-30 says, *"Jesus knew that his mission was now finished, and to fulfill Scripture he said, 'I am thirsty.' A jar of sour wine was sitting there, so they soaked a sponge in it, put it on a hyssop branch, and held it up to his lips. When Jesus had tasted it, he said, 'It is finished!' Then he bowed his head and released his spirit."* This means that Jesus fulfilled His mission for His Father; the mission of redemption had been accomplished.

His death would be the only way for us to be redeemed from our sins in order to inherit eternal life. His act of obedience and faithfulness to God brought the greatest glory to His Father.

Christ prayed for all believers during His final hours:

*I do not pray for these alone, but also for those who will believe in Me through their word; that they all may be one, as You, Father, are in Me, and I in You; that they also may be one in Us, that the world may believe that You sent Me. And the glory which You gave Me I have given them, that they may be one just as We are one: I in them, and You in Me; that they may be made perfect in one, and that the world may know that You have sent Me, and have loved them as You have loved Me.*

*Father, I desire that they also whom You gave Me may be with Me where I am, that they may behold My glory which You have given Me; for You loved Me before the foundation of the world. O righteous Father! The world has not known You, but I have known You; and these have known that You sent Me. And I have declared to them Your name, and will declare it, that the love with which You loved Me may be in them, and I in them.* (Jn 17:20-26)

From what the Scriptures are referring to, whosoever has a common belief of the truth that was received in the Word of God is to be united. As believers, we must unite in adherence to God's plan of eternal life because we are one body of Christ all sharing His life and believing in the gospel of truth. In His prayer for believers, Jesus repeatedly expressed His great desire for oneness amongst us that we may be made perfect in one. And when we reach our goal to be in heaven, not only will we see the glory that is His but we will also share it. In the meantime, while on earth and by God's Spirit living in us, we can experience His power anytime and anywhere. *"Now hope does not disappoint, because the love of God has been poured out in our hearts by the Holy Spirit who was given to us"* (Rom 5:5). God's love must be deeply rooted within our hearts because He first loved us. Thus the Holy Spirit brings life of heaven to us, giving us the assurance of our oneness in God.

As Christians, we always have heaven in our sights, but are we truly looking forward to going to heaven? Is heaven part of our hopes and dreams as Christians? We are all certain that we will die, and as believers we are also certain that Jesus will return to earth. Though we can't predict the time when Jesus will come—nor when life will come to an end—all we can do is prepare and be ready for when that time comes. Death is inevitable, and in order to be ready, we should prepare as if we will die tomorrow and plan as if we will live for a long time.

For us Christians, we should not look at death as the end of life. Instead, consider it as the finish line in your life's journey, allowing you to claim your heavenly prize. After watching some of the athletes perform their best during the recent Olympic Games, I was drawn to thinking about their grueling preparation before the event. It reminded me of our preparations as Christians. Are we preparing our lives for final judgment? If not, why not?

Romans 5:1-4 says, *"Therefore, having been justified by faith, we have peace with God through our Lord Jesus Christ, through whom also we have access by faith into this grace in which we stand, and rejoice in hope of the glory of God. And not only that, but we also glory in tribulations, knowing that tribulation produces perseverance; perseverance, character; and character, hope."* Every day is our rehearsal; some days we work hard, and some days we don't. Some days we undergo challenges, and some days we just have fun. Be reminded that all of these are parts of the process that allows God to mold us into how He wants us to be. Let us pray that when we come face to face with God, we will be awarded with a plaque with these words found in Matthew 25:21: *"Well done, good and faithful servant; you were faithful over a few things, I will make you ruler over many things. Enter into the joy of your Lord."*

We not only need to emulate Jesus' life, teachings, and examples, but also consider His death. Jesus' unfathomable death and divine resurrection depict the essential qualities of the One who saves. We should learn how to face our own death as he had. Do not fear death, but instead, learn to accept it with confidence because we shall have the gracious presence of God at death and forever. It was probably the hardest thing for me to accept when I was diagnosed with my illness (OPLL). Not only that I was likely facing an early death, but the surgery would be risky. But because of my established personal relationship with God, I had already accepted my illness with confidence, trusting that it happened for a reason. With my full trust in God, I have learned not to be overwhelmed with fear but rather overwhelmed with faith in my Savior. The fear of death or becoming paralyzed during the surgery frequently came to my mind, but I kept going back to God's Word about trusting Him always. Proverbs 3:5-6 (NKJV) says, *"Trust in the LORD with all your heart, And lean not on your own understanding; In all your ways acknowledge Him, And He shall direct your paths."*

It is so easy and convenient for people to trust themselves rather than God. Anyone can easily fall into this trap of evil. But God always meant for good things to happen in our lives as we abide in His promises and commands. Things happen for a reason, and sometimes it is far beyond our control. With my physical ailment, I thank God I came to know it early on in my life because it gave me enough time to prepare myself for the things He wants me to do. Indeed, God has already begun His good work in me, as I became able, willing, and ready to do His will. Praise His holy name!

I hope and pray that God will use this book to deliver His great message to many. I hope that the six-step process for spiritual growth outlined in this book will help redirect people to come to know and live with God. How great it would be if we could get a glimpse of our *real* home in the presence of our almighty Father.

In near-death situations, some people claimed to have caught a glimpse of heaven. That may be. Instead of focusing our attention on this, we can just read and meditate upon God's Word for His revelation to us. Yes, there is a heaven, and the Bible says our citizenship is in heaven. Living and leading a godly life will guide and direct our journey to arrive at our final, heavenly destination. We will then get our final reward of eternal life. This proves that a Christian's life has no end. Death is never the end of our life; rather, it is the beginning of a new experience of life with God. Until then, we have works to do not only for ourselves but for God and His purpose in us.

We all have missions, and our abilities to fulfill our mission depend largely on our obedience and faithfulness to God. Many things can happen during our journey, good and bad. We could die from some disease or be healed, but without any doubt, we will *all* be healed—maybe not on the earth but in heaven with the Lord. Just open the window of reality, reflect on the brevity of life, and celebrate each moment in time. Death does not go away.

We must put our tight grip upon His promises that will hold us along this rugged path. In Christ, we dwell with the One who paid for our lives; our only hope is in Him. We live because He lives. 2 Corinthians 5:8 says, *"We are confident, yes, well pleased rather to be absent from the body and to be present with the Lord."* Because we believe that heaven is a better place than the earth, we should yearn to be home with the Lord. Our solemn prayers, our unyielding commune with the living Word of God, and the indwelling presence of the Holy Spirit should be a reflection of our transparency in expressing our heavenly homesickness. Philippians 3:14 (NIV) says, *"I press on toward the goal to win the prize for which God has called me heavenward in Christ Jesus."* When the time comes that God will call us up to heaven and into His presence, we will then receive the prize that is unreachable on earth. Christlike behavior in heaven should be our ultimate goal on earth until we reach God's heavenly realm. Passing through the meandering stream of faithlessness, the rambling forest paths of an unforgiving heart, the bewildered truth of the gospel, and the winding road of loneliness, we must leave a trail of overflowing faith, interlocking bricks of hearts, the solid rock of truth, and a paved road to happiness. We call upon God to bless us in our journey toward our almighty Father in heaven.

# My Personal Conviction as a Woman of God

What an amazing God we have—if only we would allow Him to control our lives. Having been saved by Jesus' redemptive sufferings and death on the cross, we can pursue an intimate personal relationship with God. James 4:8 says, *"Draw near to God and He will draw near to you. Cleanse your hands, you sinners; and purify your hearts, you double-minded."* As we draw near to God, we become rightly related to Him. The Holy Spirit intercedes and takes our concerns before God who provides us with wisdom and understanding through our faith. As we pray and humble ourselves to God, He will enlighten our minds, cleanse our hearts, enrich our souls, and empower us to pursue godly living. That is the focus of this book, as it also relates to my personal conviction as a woman of God.

God truly convicted my heart to share this message. This is a true revelation of my personal struggle that brought sadness, anger, frustration, and hatred into my heart. It almost wrecked my family relationship and nearly derailed my path to accomplish a much-desired and godly purpose. This struggle pertains to women who battle with the leadership role in the family. *The dilemma:* when husbands do not like to lead and become uninvolved or sometimes unpredictable about their role as "head of the family." It is sad to say that this is happening to many families out there. In some situations, when left unattended, it can create disarray in the family, divorce, or infidelity. According to James Walker, "Many a woman today lives the hollow, lonely life. Bearing a constant ache in her soul, she determines to hang on, but without hope that her husband will change. She is convinced he will never take the lead in their marriage or with their children—much less develop emotional intimacy with her."[15] No matter how you look at it, the result is a dysfunctional family.

Unfortunately, this was my experience, which almost ruined my life and my family relationship. For many years, I was in a state of denial, absorbed with responsibilities, full of pride and arrogance, and most of all, God was not the center of my daily living. But these all changed when I surrendered my life to God's sovereignty and control. Our God is an awesome God, faithful and forgiving, and His love is unconditional that He made all these things available and possible for me. Indeed, God rescued me and directed my path exactly as Proverbs 3:5-7 says: "Trust in the LORD with all your heart, And lean not on your own understanding; *In all your ways acknowledge Him, And He shall direct your paths."* He showed me the only right way, His way. Isaiah 55:9 says, *"For as the heavens are higher than the earth, So are My ways higher than your ways, And My thoughts than your thoughts."*

Even from the early stages of our marriage, my husband never took the role of leadership. I was always left to make all the major decisions. At one point, I tried to convince him to be at the forefront in the decision making. Most of the time, my pleas fell on deaf ears, and I gave up and became the decision maker of the family. From financial issues to taking care of the kids, I assumed all the responsibilities myself. There were times I was labeled a "control freak" in the family, but I dismissed their case. I was not aiming to be a people pleaser. Back then, I did not have a personal relationship with the Lord, and I used to say that it was my way or the

---

15. James Walker, *Husbands Who Won't Lead & Wives Who Won't Follow* (Minneapolis, MN: Bethany House, 2000), 9.

highway. I didn't say it to be mean; I was just protecting the well-being of my family.

At first I thought that taking the role of leadership in my family would remove some of the load from my husband's shoulders. But it was too late; I had already begun to damage the relationship. I freed him from a lot of the responsibilities, and I also catered to his needs as a good wife to her husband. I have to admit, though, that my husband is a good financial provider. I am so proud of him for that. I never complained about money. However, I had concerns that he thought his responsibilities ended with bringing home the paycheck. Perhaps I was wrong, but he was not clear about a lot of things. This continued to happen for a long time. Determined to make the relationship better, I ignored the matter and didn't make a big deal out of it. I was strong in my disposition but really didn't know what was going on in my husband's mind.

Ten years into the marriage, I noticed that things began to change, but it still didn't bother me, knowing that my husband was not very serious about our family life. Sometimes he could be funny; yet he could also be adamant about some things that didn't fit his agenda. On the other hand, I had a tendency to be too serious about life and very outspoken. We always seemed to be heading in the opposite direction in our relationship. In spite of our differences, we managed to stay well for the most part. During those days, nothing seemed to sway me in all that I was determined to accomplish in life. I was supportive of whatever things my husband strived to do. In our relationship, I tried to fix things, while it seemed that my husband derailed the process with his bad judgment.

My husband was very complacent about me taking the lead in our relationship. It didn't bother him. Until one day, an anonymous harassment letter came in the mail, and it was addressed to me. It was wicked, cruel, and demeaning, and it shocked every ounce of my body. Stunned with great disbelief, I cried immensely. I began to lose control of my emotions. With a trembling voice I blurted, "How can people be this cruel, insensitive, and heartless?" It was hard for me even to imagine how somebody could write mean and evil words to anyone; yet it was actually happening to me. Extremely puzzled and disturbed by this letter, I began to examine things around me. I kept asking myself, *Who are my enemies, and why are they doing this?* Some of the provocative remarks were about my husband, but mostly, it was directed at me. They said I was fat, ugly, didn't deserve this or that, and on and on. I tried to let it go at first, but things began to escalate, and it posed a threat to me and my family.

I would like to think that this person was crazy because I didn't have any recollection of being mean or hurtful to anyone. I was clueless as to who wrote this letter, and it was hard for me to even comprehend. It felt like it was never ending. The harassing letters and obscene packages kept coming. I was enraged and infuriated by the whole situation, and it brought extreme sadness and anger into my heart. Many attempts were made to trace these letters and packages but to no avail. I became very worrisome. Very often I blurted out, "Who could be my enemy? Somebody is purposely provoking and invading my privacy!" Disheartened by this situation, I began to refocus my anger on my husband. Despite my worries and fears, he appeared to be heartless and without empathy. As my worry escalated, we began to argue more. I felt that no one could be trusted. It was very noticeable how my husband stayed calm about everything. It felt like I was in a constant panic attack, and my husband would not react. I had no idea what was happening.

More peculiar things happened while those letters kept coming. Every night for a month or two the telephone just kept on ringing every five minutes with no response at the other end. This happened mostly during the night when my husband was at work. Indeed, it was very nerve-racking. Shaken by the whole ordeal, it was beginning to control my normal life. Still, my husband was calm every time I complained about the constant phone calls. At the peak of my anger and frustration, I was determined to confront my husband once again.

Pain engulfed my whole being. There were days of pure agony, as I wept until dawn. My heart was filled with anger and frustration, and my mind wandered. I thought, *What do I do now?* Questions left unanswered, tears just rolled down my cheeks. This is how it was for me, day in and day out. Suddenly, the shocking news was spilled: my husband admitted to having an extra-marital affair. It felt like a sharp knife had just penetrated my chest, and I screamed for help with all of my might.

To make matters worse, I felt like everyone was against me. *Who can I trust? Whose shoulder can I cry on? Who will rescue me?* I had no one. Going back to work after a short leave of absence devastated me more. Pretending nothing happened was not my style. I couldn't hide my true feelings. Every day as I stepped out the door, I felt like I had to wear a mask over my whole being. I was not me. I was alive yet didn't feel like I even existed. My soul was grieving, and my heart was screaming for help. Very often I wanted to shout to the whole world, "I am not the person I was!" For a week, there was a feeling of numbness in my entire body, almost as if I was hit by lightning that ignited a flame in my heart, melting every cell inside me. There were many sleepless nights, just as there were many times I wished never to wake up again.

At the mercy of my sister, she invited my husband to live with them in Guam. I had to let go of him so I could have some time to myself. In spite of him being gone, I continued to dwell on my miseries, reckoning what went wrong, why it happened, and why me. My sister suggested what might have gone wrong in the relationship. "You did not give him any responsibilities, and you freed his mind to become preoccupied." I was pretty naïve about the whole arrangement, thinking it would be good for him, as much as it would be for me, as a good wife to her husband. I didn't know what to think or what to believe any longer, and I shut the door of my heart for anyone to come in.

It was hard for me to believe that my husband could do such a thing. I thought I was doing a good job for the family by relieving him from all the worries and responsibilities of the household. We were both clamoring to the opposite direction in our lifestyles and thought processes. Inflamed with much anger, I asked him, "How could you do this to me? You betrayed me and your children. You're a liar and a deceitful man." I wanted to throw all of my hurtful words into his face. All he could do was say sorry for his bad behavior.

It was more than two years before he could come back home for good, and while he was gone, I became more determined to handle the family function. Although I used to blame myself for what had happened, I soon recognized that it wasn't all my fault. I had to free up my guilt; otherwise, things could have been worse. Thinking that I had given all my time—practically my whole life—to my family made me realize I had nothing left for me there. Until one day when my Lord and Savior rescued me and showed me that I had everything.

This is my prayer for deliverance:

> *If our enemy strikes us*
> *God will intercede with us*
> *In time of adversity and*
> *In time of affliction*
> *He will take vengeance for us*
>
> *Though our pain seems perpetual*
> *And our wounds incurable*
> *God will surely restore us*

*No enemy will prevail*
*God will fight for us to save us*

*God delivers us from the wicked*
*He will redeem us from our sins. Amen.*

Shortly thereafter, I also realized that everything happens for a reason. Indeed, my husband's issue of infidelity was just one part of the problem. There were more unresolved, preexisting issues of the past. According to James Walker, "The truth of the matter is, today's man has found his role radically redefined from that of his father or grandfather. It is difficult for men today to even understand the uniqueness of their God-given position in the family."[16] I was therefore more intrigued than challenged by my husband's behavior. Although I may never understand *why*, all I could do was cry and murmur, *What was he thinking?*

Adding to the turmoil caused by my husband, people around me were on a constant lookout to my family affairs, making unsolicited comments and sending harassing letters that were demeaning, judgmental, and filled with threats. As I neared the end of my rope, God rescued me. Wholeheartedly I accepted Jesus as my Lord and Savior, and I started building my personal relationship with Him. The harassment continued for over a decade. It would be another six years before it came to a complete halt. I went to the police about the matter, but nothing happened. Determined to mend my nearly wrecked marital relationship, I decided to bring the matter to God. Mystified by the cruelty of these people, I derailed their transgression and repelled it with the power of forgiveness.

This whole ordeal simply brought me closer to the Lord who strengthened me so I could handle life head on.

16. James Walker, *Husbands Who Won't Lead & Wives Who Won't Follow* (Minneapolis, MN: Bethany House, 2000) 10.

The enormity of my problems could have easily hindered my path to fulfill God's purpose. I could have never pursued my godly mission of leading people to God.

A husband who won't lead and remains uninvolved with their role as head of the family is a great challenge for wives. Every situation is different. Therefore, it is my intention that by sharing this publicly it will open up many people's heart to acknowledge and become aware of its existence and its impact on the marriage relationship. My goal is to give hope and encouragement. I deeply and wholeheartedly pray for women who struggle with leadership roles in the household to seek guidance; there is a way out of the mess. One way. God's way.

Like any organization, a family needs a leader; otherwise, it could become chaotic, and the tendency for the family to fall apart is very likely to happen. It is in the basic nature of man to be the leader of the family, and this is very true in a traditional Christian family. If we read God's Word, in Ephesians 5:22-31 it tells us about marriage as a sacred reflection of Christ and the church. From these Scriptures, we begin to clearly understand the true meaning of the husband as the leader of the family with the wife submitting to her husband.

> *Wives, submit to your own husbands, as to the Lord. For the husband is head of the wife, as also Christ is head of the church; and He is the Savior of the body. Therefore, just as the church is subject to Christ, so let the wives be to their own husbands in everything. Husbands, love your wives, just as Christ also loved the church and gave Himself for her, that He might sanctify and cleanse her with the washing of water by the word, that He might present her to Himself a glorious church, not having spot or wrinkle or any such thing, but that she should be holy and*

*without blemish. So husbands ought to love their own wives as their own bodies; he who loves his wife loves himself. For no one ever hated his own flesh, but nourishes and cherishes it, just as the Lord does the church. For we are members of His body, of His flesh and of His bones. "For this reason a man shall leave his father and mother and be joined to his wife, and the two shall become one flesh." This is a great mystery, but I speak concerning Christ and the church. Nevertheless let each one of you in particular so love his own wife as himself, and let the wife see that she respects her husband.*

Let's backtrack to what was said in Ephesians 5:21: *"Submitting to one another in the fear of God."* In this verse, Paul declared, unequivocally, that true believers are to be humble and submissive to one another, which is foundational to all relationships. The Scripture also says that no believer is superior over any other believer, and Galatians 3:28 affirms this: *"There is neither male or female for you are all one in Christ Jesus."* Therefore, between husband and wife, having an established relationship in marriage as one, the Christian wife's submission is *not* to the command of the husband; instead, she willingly and lovingly offers herself to the man whom God has placed over her. It is an obedient act to God regardless of her husband's personal worthiness or spiritual condition. Similarly, the husband's role in being a leader is not only God ordained but also a reflection of Christ's loving head of the church. Divine love seeks for purity, and husbands ought to love their wives with the desire that she become conformed to Christ. So, then, a husband who loves his wife as himself brings great blessings to himself from her and from God. Marriage becomes a sacred reflection of the great mystery of union between Christ and the church.

Indeed, if the husband is to assume the biblical role of leadership in the family, it has to be the kind of leadership that is mandated to us by Jesus' teachings, His examples of leadership, and the instructions of God's Word. Leadership is not about domination, power, or control; otherwise, the Bible will be greatly misunderstood—an abomination to God. Unfortunately, the battle of control, power, and domination does exist, which can leave the wife in the dark, living a lonely life, bearing a hardened heart, or suffering from an aching soul with little or no hope that her husband will change.

This battle of control between husband and wife is against what the Bible has to say about male and female being equal in the eyes of the Lord. Very often, my husband used to tell me that as long as I didn't bother him, he was fine with the arrangement. For the most part, I did what I had to do—focus on my children and the family's well-being. There were signs of insecurity in my husband, but I ignored them.

According to Walker, "A woman can take over." But here is the big question: is she *really* in control? Walker says,

> Men who are faced with constant criticism give up. The friction they find when they come home drives them deeper into the sports page and ties them more passively than ever to TV. Most men will do anything to avoid confrontation. When confronted at home with never-ending conflict, a man will appear to sound the retreat. For as long as he continued to sit and not respond to her demands, he remained in control. She could rant, rave, rage, beg, plead or promise, but the immovable object was still the center of everyone's attention. He was passively in complete authority. This withdrawn, passive behavior in men can be essentially a real struggle for control. The passive

man can still, effectively, manage his own life. This type of control, however, removes him from the family. His wife may view his removal as necessary for the orderly function of the home, but what is necessary for the short term will be devastating to the marriage in the long term.[17]

This was exactly what I felt happened between my husband and me for a long time. I was labeled the "control freak" and considered the bad guy in the marriage, but I was not. I had good intentions in the relationship. I was just too naïve to even confront my true feelings about a lot of things, and I shouldn't have ignored my husband's indifference. The negative long-term effect of "letting go" or "ignoring" my husband's silent treatment did not cross my mind. I was in denial of any existing problem, and the absorption of responsibilities was my escape from the whole ordeal.

As a result of the betrayal, I felt that I could never trust him again, and it created a wall between us. I almost gave up on the relationship, but the more I thought about it, the more I was drawn to my Father. Oftentimes, God reminded me that He was the only one who could fix everything for me. All I needed to do was to pray and trust God. So I did. This was my prayer for God's mercy:

> *O Lord my strength and my fortress*
> *My refuge in the day of my affliction*
> *Forgive my worthlessness and unprofitable things*
> *Mighty is Your name, the Lord of hosts. Amen.*

During my separation from my husband, God's grace led me to my healing process. God granted me the power to forgive as I was committed to walk in faith with Him. In my husband's absence, I learned to forgive him. Reminded by

17. James Walker, *Husbands Who Won't Lead & Wives Who Won't Follow* (Minneapolis, MN: Bethany House, 2000) 29–30.

this cliché, "Absence makes the heart grow fonder," I began to long for his presence. I redirected my attention by getting actively involved in a local church. I was so blessed to be surrounded by godly women. Then there was a time when my husband needed to undergo surgery, and he had to come home. While at home recovering from the surgery, he also accepted Jesus as his Lord and Savior. In no time, he decided to come back home for good. We both planned for a good start.

We vowed to have God as the center of our life together. It sure eased a lot of the pain and suffering, but unfortunately, he was still not interested in his role as the head of the household. He didn't show interest, but he seemed agreeable with almost everything that I wanted to do. It was as if we were back to square one, only this time, he was more careful of his actions and judgment calls. He was a little bit more focused on the kids' needs and some household chores.

I decided to go back to school and finish my MBA. This enabled me to change my career path. I believe that this all happened for a reason because I sought God earnestly in my life. Going back to school may have been a way of redirecting my worrisome thoughts. I constantly meditated on this passage in Matthew because if I didn't focus my mind on God, then I would begin to worry again: *"But seek first the kingdom of God and His righteousness, and all these things shall be added to you"* (Mt 6:33). Rather than worrying, I channeled my attention and hopes to God that He would take care of all my problems, just as I also hoped to win my husband into God's kingdom.

Our life began to pick up again, although my hopes for him to lead the family did not happen. However, seeing some improvements in him was reassuring. Walking with God and making Him my priority slowly healed the pain and suffering. However, a rallying cry in my heart often distracted my moments with God. As I prayed, I always wanted to cry out, *Where is my husband in all of these?* With intense prayer seeking God's help, I murmured, "Lord, please change my husband's heart for my sake and for my family's sake." For a long time, nothing happened.

The feeling of everyday disappointments enveloped my soul. I felt that although my husband received the Lord, it didn't seem to matter to him as much as I had hoped. I had to express my discontentment that he might have just been trying to be good in order to please me and to keep the relationship alive. More arguments followed, but this time, it was all about his walk with God. Talking to him about my faith seemed to irritate him. He ignored anything and everything that concerned my plans to do ministry work. I had to drag him to go to church every Sunday. But I didn't give up on him. God was always my strength, and each time I had issues with my husband, I called unto God and prayed more intensely with my deepest longing for his heart to change.

My husband was skeptical of me going to Bible study, but I did it anyway. Oftentimes, I asked God to forgive me of my disobedience to my husband. Looking back, I recognize that although he had some issues, I also had mine. While it was true that I had all the intentions to serve God in any capacity I could, I failed God because of my disobedience in my actions and reactions toward my husband. Matthew 7:1 says, *"Judge not, that you be not judged."* Jesus was telling me never to think or make a value judgment. I could have been easily defied by self-righteousness, egotistical judgment, and unmerciful condemnation. I prayed to God and asked Him to forgive me.

As I continued serving God, I was also doing well as a financial advisor. A colleague used to ask me what my secret was, and very often I just shared my faith and trust in God. *"But seek first the kingdom of God and His righteousness, and all these things shall be added to you"* (Mt 6:33). This Scripture reminds us to seek His righteousness. That instead of longing after the things of this world, we ought to hunger for the things of God. As a financial advisor, with my compassion for people and my earnest desire to help people in their financial planning, it draws me even closer to God. I used to pray this prayer, which made me become more passionate in serving God:

*Tess' Prayer*

*Heavenly Father:*
*The day I came to know You was just the beginning,*
*Of something new that I look forward to every morning,*
*There were days that I didn't know what to do,*
*But You were always there to remind me of You.*

*Then one day came a new vision for me to explore,*
*Helping people with their financial situations and more,*
*My compassion became a passion for everyday living,*
*Again, Lord, You added more reasons worth believing.*

*That just helping my clients was not the end,*
*But teaching Bible study could gain a friend,*
*Witnessing to people about Your love, mercy, and grace,*
*That You suffered and died on the cross for us to be saved.*

*My Lord and Savior, as Your purpose has unfolded,*
*Through the writing of this book it should be told,*
*That people must account for their lives as they journey heavenward,*
*For Yours is the kingdom, the power, and glory to the whole wide world.*
*Amen.*

Immensely captivated by God's love, I continued to pursue the great work He began into my life. Determined to be obedient to God's command, I started witnessing and sharing the gospel with others. At this point, I wanted to witness to my immediate family. My husband was against my plans to witness to his mother, who was very ill at that time, but I persisted. Doing things like this simply irritated him more, and I felt like we were growing apart each time I was determined to do ministry work. But I learned to be stronger each day as I sought God into my life and vowed not to ever give up on him. We both committed to doing our daily devotions, but it was a struggle for him. I did start to see some changes in him. Still, his idea of leading the family was not something he hoped for. I suppose he was not comfortable or did not have the confidence. But I leaned on what the Bible says, not in my time but in God's. In 1 Timothy 6:15 it says, *"Which He will manifest in His own time."*

With my deepest longings to understand all the things around me and my earnest desire for God's manifestation into my life, I spent countless hours studying, learning, and meditating upon God's Word. Determined to know more of Jesus, His teachings, and His examples, I decided to enroll in a doctoral program—biblical studies with an emphasis in biblical leadership. All the hours I spent studying God's Word brought light into my husband's life, as he slowly opened his heart to see the truth about God. Praise the Lord because it became an instrument for my husband to see Jesus, and he could now walk and grow in faith with Him.

Indeed, my structured study was very rewarding in so many ways as it already touched my husband's heart to be drawn closer to God. It also enhanced my vision to take my missionary project into a higher level of God's calling. A very purposeful and godly missionary project unfolded just after I received my doctorate. This was another call to godly living manifested by God, just as I always longed and prayed for. Psalm 138:8 says, *"The LORD will work out his plans for my life—for your faithful love, O LORD, endures forever. Don't abandon me, for you made me."* God is true with all His promises, and His plans are real. God's manifestation into my husband's life was becoming visible to my husband. He became very supportive of my ministry. So now, I could claim this Scripture: *"I have fought the good fight, I have finished the race, I have kept the faith"* (2 Tm 4:7).

A few months before my graduation, I had the chance to visit Israel for a study tour. Accompanied by my husband and my daughter, it was a great learning experience. Little did I know that this experience would become another big step to my husband's spiritual growth. In addition, God convicted my daughter's heart. She then expressed her desire to serve the Lord. Within two months, she quit her job to study evangelism. Recently, she completed her mission in Turkey and was scheduled to leave for another mission. God's merciful and powerful direction was amazing, and all I could do was thank the Lord for His guidance and provision in my life. My daughter's desire to serve the Lord was testified by her obedience to this passage in Mark 8:34: *"When He had called the people to Himself, with His disciples also, He said to them, 'Whoever desires to come after Me, let him deny himself, and take up his cross, and follow Me.'"*

It was before our trip to Israel that I was diagnosed with OPLL. As shocking as the news was, we all took it very well. Our strong faith in God continued to hold us up. Despite circumstances like this, our perspectives in life changed in the way we looked at problems. My husband and I may not be on the same speed of spiritual growth, but by God's mercy we're maintaining our strong faith in God. This Scripture began to minister to me: *"If you diligently heed the voice of the LORD your God and do what is right in His sight, give ear to His commandments and keep all His statutes, I will put none of the diseases on you which I have brought on the Egyptians. For I am the LORD who heals you"* (Ex 15:26).

While we were in Israel, my ailment never even bothered us that much. We just prayed earnestly to God for healing and direction. Our everyday activities in Israel were all about praising Jesus, studying His life, visiting holy places, and reliving everything that happened to Jesus. We explored all the significant places during Jesus' time. What I witnessed during the trip was reassuring. I felt like Jesus was telling me, *Everything will be OK.* It was confirmed that God wanted me to relive how Jesus suffered compared to what I was going through. I began to lift everything to God for divine healing.

Despite my neurosurgeon's recommendation for surgery, I had to delay the process to undertake a missionary project to the Philippines. Jesus said in Matthew 6:34, *"Therefore do not worry about tomorrow, for tomorrow will worry about its own things. Sufficient for the day is its own trouble."* What a reassuring passage from Jesus, I thought. God promises His grace for tomorrow and every day thereafter, but I believe that He only gives grace as needed. I learned not to dwell on what tomorrow brings.

While we were sailing on the Sea of Galilee, I pretended that Jesus was with us next to the boat walking on the water. With my eyes tightly closed, I painted His picture in my heart with His hand outstretched as if He was saying, *Come follow me and walk with me.* I cried quietly. Indeed, it was a very emotional and unforgettable experience.

Coming back home from Israel was peaceful and refreshing. I couldn't get over talking about it and was still awed with the whole experience. My daughter opened up and said to me, "Mom, I have been earning a good amount of money since I finished college. I haven't served the Lord, and I want to do it now." I paused for a moment before I could say, "Are you sure of what you're doing?" Only to realize that I was persecuting her just like how my husband used to question me. I gave her my blessing, and she went on to her plans.

In the meantime, it was very unusual seeing my husband very responsive and participative in the household chores. I saw a lot of changes in him. God was truly working in his heart. Now it was time for me to refocus on myself. I was awakened by the truth that although my husband was to be blamed for all his wrong judgment calls, I should also take part of the blame. Just then, I repented and asked God to forgive me. I believe that I could have done things to alleviate the pain and suffering and could have avoided the prolonged damage that was inflicted. I was truly touched by this Scripture: *"But those who wait on the LORD shall renew their strength; they shall mount up with wings like eagles, They shall run and not be weary, They shall walk and not faint"* (Is 40:31).

In studying Walker's book, I realized it was unfortunate that I was not able to take time to understand my husband's indifference early on in the relationship. Though I could already sense some of his passivity and uninvolved feelings, I still ignored them. Ignoring the problem was one thing, but also enabling it was another thing. Perhaps it was easier to think nothing was wrong. So I took all the family responsibilities onto myself instead of effectively ministering to my husband. It was the most regrettable decision I made.

Marked by confidence in Walker's recommendation and pressing on toward restoring our relationship, I realized how much we must be rightly related to God. Needless to say, this was my strong conviction. For a very long time after I accepted Jesus into my heart, I was totally committed to helping my husband emerge into his God-given role. During that much-awaited time, I became intimate in my personal relationship with God. In Him I drew my strength, in Him I learned how to forgive, and in Him I was provided with wisdom and understanding. While God was working in my husband's heart, God gave me the deepest longings to serve

Him as I made myself able, willing, and ready to do His will. In 2 Corinthians 12:19 it says, *"My grace is sufficient for you, for My strength is made perfect in weakness."* God's amazing grace, His mercy and compassion, and His unconditional love brought a new beginning, a new life, and renewed perspectives, and most of all, He restored our relationship.

The following Scripture ministered to me many times: *"Ask, and it will be given to you; seek, and you will find; knock, and it will be opened to you. For everyone who asks receives, and he who seeks finds, and to him who knocks it will be opened"* (Mt 7:7-8). We can't have discernment without divine counsel from God. With God's unconditional love, He gave me every ounce of strength I needed to survive in this whole ordeal. God gave me the power to forgive myself, my husband, and everyone who wronged me. His reassurance to follow my heart's desire to serve Him made it all happen. Psalm 37:4 says, *"Delight yourself also in the LORD, And He shall give you the desires of your heart."* He paved the way to take me into a greater calling. God is always there for you and me.

First Kings 8:57 says, *"May the LORD our God be with us, as He was with our fathers. May He not leave us nor forsake us."* I cannot begin to fathom how my life could have been without God in my life. God gave me enough truth to understand Him and be responsible but also enough mystery to become dependent on Him. I thank and praise God for all of these things, as I express them in this concluding prayer:

*Blessed are You, Lord God, our Father*
*For in You is the greatness and power*
*For in You is the heaven and the earth*
*In Your hand is power to give strength*
*In Your hand is light to our path*
*Your grace, mercy, and love we all received from You*
*You are exalted, for riches and honor come from You*
*You reign over all, and we thank You and praise You. Amen.*